ROSES and RAINBOWS

By the same author:

Other Days Around Me

ROSES and RAINBOWS

FLORENCE MARY McDOWELL

Illustrated by Rowel Friers

Foreword by Professor J C Beckett

Blackstaff Press   Belfast

Published by Blackstaff Press Limited, 16 Donegall Square
South, Belfast BT1 5JF
with the assistance of the Arts Council for Northern Ireland.

First edition   1972
Second edition 1974

SBN 85640 075 0 (Hardback)
SBN 85640 074 2 (Paperback)

Printed in Northern Ireland by Belfast Litho Printers Limited.

'. . . . . I now
Remember
The days of roses but as a dream.'

James Clarence Mangan

'Erin, the Tear and the Smile in thine eyes
Blend, like the Rainbow that hangs in the sky.'

Thomas Moore

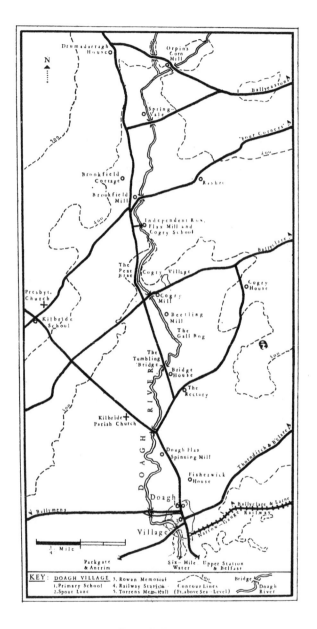

Doagh Village

Foreword

I still remember the pleasure and excitement with which I read Mrs McDowell's earlier book, *Other Days Around Me*, the story of a County Antrim childhood in the last years of Queen Victoria's reign. The excitement did not lie in the events themselves, but in the verve with which they were recorded. A whole countryside was brought to life, as seen through the sharp yet friendly eyes of a little girl, who stored her memory with the casual occurrences of everyday life. Here, in *Roses and Rainbows*, the story of the family at the Bridge House is continued. Mary, now in the process of growing up, is a Monitress at the National School; but she still has the same enquiring mind, the same eye for a situation, the same ear for a bit of racy talk and, above all, the same freshness of outlook that can make even the commonplace memorable.

For the social historian, Mrs McDowell's books will long remain a useful source of information - Mary's experiences as a Monitress, for example, tell us a good deal about the educational system of the time that did not get into the official reports. Even the reader who would disown any special interest in history will learn, perhaps without realising it, a good deal about the past. At the least, he will learn something about the life of the countryside before it was opened up by the motor car and the bus, and at a time when a journey by train was, for most country people, a rare event. And it may do him some good to discover that the people of those days could entertain themselves without the aid of radio or television, and were seldom at a loss for something to talk about, though the news of the world was not brought nightly to their living rooms.

But though these books may fairly be regarded as historical documents, they are also something more. The scene is a narrow corner of County Antrim; the actors are the ordinary

7

people of the neighbourhood going about their ordinary business; but the underlying themes are as broad as human life itself. All is simply and unpretentiously told. Mrs McDowell has the rare art of being natural and she allows her episodes to produce their own effects, without intrusive stage management.

But there are things here that no reader is likely to forget - the reading of Pappy's Will; the conversation overheard at a wake; the family reciting The Litany in Aunt Laetitia's bedroom; Mary at the Bazaar, playing the part of a colleen. All this will have a special significance for Irish readers; but the essential appeal is universal. Times and circumstances change; but everywhere and always, as in Mrs McDowell's pages, human experience seems to fluctuate between the tear and the smile.

Professor of Irish History,   J C Beckett
Department of Modern History,
The Queen's University,
Belfast

Acknowledgments

I thank not only the many friends and acquaintances who have contributed in some way to the making of this book, but also the readers of its predecessor, *Other Days Around Me*, whose wonderful kindness made it all worthwhile. I was grateful for the many good wishes I received, along with helpful hints and further suggestions. If I were to act on all of these, I should be occupied in writing for the next thirty years at least!

Instead, I ask you to accept the successor to *Other Days* with at least as much kindness as you did that first book.

I thank the following for specific help in elucidating and cross-checking several points, for dogged work in typing and for individual research: Mrs Thomas Moore ('Little Sister'); Miss M J S Dugan ('Moxie'); Miss I W M McDowell; Miss Jennie McDowell; Mrs M P Langhammer; Mrs Eileen McCormick; Mrs Maisie Crawford; Eric Langhammer; Mr Hugh Speers; Rev Michael Kelly, PP; Mr A E McClean; Mrs Mary Boyd; Mrs Molly Tweed; Miss Bessie Blair; Mr Patrick Dickson of Hawlmark, and Mr Ewart Craig, Town Clerk, Ballyclare.

I should like to take this opportunity also of thanking those who, in days past, helped me get started in my 'new' career - Mrs Jeanne Cooper Foster, Mr Sam Hanna Bell, Mr Pat Riddell and that best of illustrators, Mr Rowel Friers. But for their great disinterested kindness to a complete stranger, I should never have succeeded in getting anywhere, I am quite sure.

I thank my daughters Iza and Joan, who have done much of the drudgery without hope of the glory. I consider that I have corrected quite enough books in my lifetime without starting that particular caper again. So theirs has been the unselfish work of construction, correction and criticism.

Finally, I say a proud 'Thank you' to Professor J C Beckett, who has lent his name and great scholarship to the Foreword of

Roses and Rainbows. I do hope that I shall, at the very least, not disgrace him.

Crawfordstown House,   Florence Mary McDowell
Doagh
1969-1972

Chapter 1

It was six o'clock in the morning. Alfred unlocked the back door and stepped out into the farm-yard. He stood quite still and looked towards the risen August sun behind the hedge of the Big Field. Sleepily, he stretched his tall, thin eighteen-year-old body and went for the milking pails. The day's work at Bridge House was beginning.

Upstairs, still abed, Mary and Little Sister awoke to the clanking of the buckets. They tensed muscles and relaxed them, turning restlessly in the over-warm bed. Mary moved her head so that, through sleepy half-open lids she could see her Text of Consolation, framed above the bed, all among gilded white lilies - 'Casting all your care upon Him, for He careth for you.' Care? Her eyes opened wide and sudden. Today was the day. Today the new School Year would begin. Today Mary would start school too, like the others. But today, for the first time, she would be that strange hybrid teacher-pupil, a Monitress. Her heart jumped and raced. She threw back the bed clothes and ran to let the cream holland blinds fly to the window tops.

A beautiful morning. A pet day. She turned to the fat brass bed and ruthlessly shook Little Sister awake.

'Get up,' said Mary. 'Come on. Get up quick. I'll have to button you up and if you're not ready this morning I won't wait, so get out of that bed. Now.'

She sluiced water into the basin from the flowered ewer. Mary's professional life was about to begin.

Already Lennox was downstairs. He was older than Mary and younger than Alfred. A tidy youth, he had washed and dressed neatly and was now preparing breakfast. The pot of oatmeal porridge on the range had jellied overnight and was still a little warm. Alfred had kindled the bright fire before going to milk. Now Lennox put on a kettle of clean spring water to boil, and by it set the iron frying pan to heat. Within his limited repertoire of dishes, the boy cooked excellently. Over the house there still lay the shadowy grief of Pappy's recent death. But, despite the shadow, Lennox began the day happily enough with no thought of the morrow. The morrow would surely take care of itself. It always had done. He sang pleasantly to himself as he turned the sizzling bacon.

Now Mary, almost dressed, gave Little Sister a final pull by the heels so that the child decided to arise lest worse befall. She slid slowly down the side of the high bed, her nightdress rucking up, her warm bare feet meeting cool linoleum. She pattered to one of the west facing windows. Her sleepy brown eyes peered shortsightedly at the fresh and shadowed summer garden below. Yawning, she scratched her bare stomach and pulled the calico over her head. Daintily she dabbled her fingers in Mary's washing water, rubbing the middle of her face with wet hands and dry towel. While you are still just a Little Sister, such a toilet may well suffice. Half dressed, Little Sister's day, too, was beginning. She whistled, as was her wont, jumping the stairs two at a time and sliding the last lap down the bannisters.

Mary had run down one short flight of stairs from her landing and up the opposite short flight to the boys' landing. Good; Frederick her younger brother, had almost finished dressing, eating as he did so a provident crust carefully stored from the night before. He masticated rapidly and dressed with equal speed. In spite of school beginning today, the world was sure to be full of surprises, happier surprises than those he had yet known. It was a very beautiful day. As the smell of frying bacon teased his nostrils, his mouth watered and he hurried to meet the attractions of breakfast.

Across the landing from the boys' room, Mary waited for a moment outside her Aunt's closed door. Aunt Laetitia never rose for breakfast. She had, instead, her own particular ritual to perform. As though the wall were transparent, Mary could see her elderly Aunt sitting up in bed, a shawl draped over her head like an enveloping tent to enclose her Cure. Every morning at five o'clock Aunt Laetitia awoke to gasping lungs and a tight chest. She was well prepared for this daily burden. With her ever-tremulous fingers she opened the tin of Potter's Asthma Cure and spooned a little of the greenish-yellow powder into a saucer. A lighted match touched to the powder produced billows of acrid fumes. Aunt Laetitia drew the smoking saucer within her tent. Together, she and the saucer would commune until the racking, hacking coughs induced by the Cure should have 'cleared her pipes' sufficiently to begin their new day.

In the pleasant kitchen immediately below Aunt Laetitia's bedroom, the five young orphans gathered to break their healthy fasts. Mary meditated sadly as she set the table. The youngsters still sat at the labourers' table, leaving empty that other where Pappy and Aunt Laetitia had used to breakfast together in happier days. A little out of date, a coloured calendar, with a large red uniformed Lord Bobs surrounded by such lesser lights of the recent war as Baden-Powell, Kitchener, Redvers Buller and Mary's own Sir George White, looked down on Pappy's eternally empty place.

Pappy had been dead a month now. His children grieved deeply for him. They missed his kind gentleness, his deep if sometimes ineffectual interest in their lives. As their Rock, they now had Aunt Laetitia. Mary felt that her Aunt might well prove to have more of the adamant than the safe stronghold in her character as Rock. Time was very soon to tell, as that day Pappy's Will would be read and explained to his children and his sister.

Mary had more immediate worries to face as she tried in vain to swallow the eggs and bacon that Lennox had prepared with such loving care. She had to start in Cogry Mills National School as Monitress this very morning. She was a small thin fifteen, dressed in dyed black mourning for Pappy that still smelt of Aunt Laetitia's dye-bath. So thin was she that her skirt had to be secretly pinned under the waistband to ensure that the decencies would be preserved. She chewed gloomily, wishing with all her heart that she had paid more attention to the work of Monitresses she had known in her mere pupillage. She made a determined effort to shrug off the menace of the morning. Outside, the sun was shining with early brilliance on dewy roses and clematis. The long shadows of the trees pointed towards the Parish Church. In the sparkling birth of this new day, there was so much beginning that Mary felt she could scarcely bear it. Nonetheless, through grief and worry came brief flashes of pleasure in the bright world outside.

Alfred was the first to push back his chair. He was the man of the house now and there was much to do. He was tall, good-looking, with dark, curly hair and deep brown eyes like those of

13

the gay little Mother who had died so many years ago. He was clever too, the brilliant one of the family. Mary often felt it was a pity that he had left school to come home to look after the farm. She looked after him as he went out by the back door through the morning sunshine to his beloved stables.

Lennox rose with Mary to clear the table. They filled the sink from the range boiler and commanded the two younger children to bring the rest of the dirty dishes. With expedition all was soon clean and neat, the dishes sitting to drain until Aunt Laetitia should come down later to an empty house.

Alfred, re-entering, cast a languid eye over his two young brothers at Mary's instigation. They looked clean enough to him.

Mary stepped out, serious and determined, on the tree arched road leading from the Bridge House towards Cogry School. Like playful squaws, the two children frolicked a yard behind. She paid them no attention. Her mind was taken up with the ordeal before her. The Master, Mr McNally, was renowned as a martinet. Mary knew this quite well. She had had to spend six months in this alien school to qualify for a Monitress-ship there. With Little Sister and Frederick now accompanying her, she did not feel so utterly lonely, though it was more than possible that they would prove more liability than asset. She hoped fervently, much as she loved them, that neither would be in the class that would be her first hurdle.

Up the tree lined road they went, past the Cogry cross roads where the fiddler used to play for dancing; over the Peat Brae with the river gurgling far below; on past Betsy Girvan's cottage with its brilliant knot-garden; up the hill to the Independent Lane. Here the trio turned right, down the narrow loanin paved with cinders and clinkers from the Cogry Mill boilers, over a rickety wooden bridge spanning the children's river, and on to the cassie in front of the school.

Scutch mill, school and row of tiny cottages formed one unbroken line. Set far back as they were from the County Road by the length of the lane, they should have provided ideally safe surroundings for small children. Instead, they were a snare and a delusion. Snare was the proximity of the river (fifteen feet below the level of the cassie and without bank or guard-rail) and of the leats, sluices and dams of the spinning mill. Delusion was the combination of the highly inflammable scutch mill attached to the school building, and of the great wooden wheel that attracted every child to its plashing slats turning and turning above an abyss of deep water.

14

The cindered cassie before the school was already swarming with children. Everyone was early. It was the first morning. It was unlikely that any other morning of the year would pass without at least one late comer. Mary hesitated. Frederick and Little Sister ran off to scream and jostle in high animal spirits with the other children. But their elder sister did not know what to do. She was neither pupil nor teacher, but a little of both. Even as she waited, the Master appeared in the porch at the scutch end of the school, bell in hand. He smiled at Mary with some kindness and beckoned her over. As she moved hesitantly towards her teaching life, some children fell back to let her pass. They looked solemnly at her solid black. They knew what it meant. She felt a moment's gratitude for their consideration and hoped it would last. Each of them was taller than herself!

If Mary had only realised how easy the first day was to prove, she would have had no worries. The whole day was taken up with getting children sorted into their new classes for the year beginning the first day of August in the year of our Lord, nineteen hundred and three. As well as being sorted into classes, the children all had to be provided with the new books appropriate to their new classes. So much did this business of Class and Book become entwined that one word was often used as a substitute for the other. Thus pupils might say they were in the Third Book, or even proudly, 'through the Books.' This meant that they had got through the top (then the Sixth) class. The school was composed of Junior Infants, Middle Infants, Senior Infants, and the classes First to Sixth. A strange hesitation took place in the Fifth class which suddenly divided into two - a year for First Fifth and a year for Second Fifth. Later the classes would run straight through from First to Seventh. Later still, they would become Standards.

This word was not without significance. The educational system became, at the hands of Civil Servants, simple but preposterous. Every child, half-timer or no, was to progress at the same rate. There would be no brilliant children, no stupid children, no dullards, no slow-coaches, no late developers. Certainly no tired, worn, hungry or over-worked children. There would be only Pupils and Standards. It would not be necessary for a Standard to fit a Pupil. Any teacher worth his salt should by some means be able to ensure that each Pupil fitted the Standard. This delusion was to persist for half a century.

Fortunately, when Mary started to learn her trade the day of

Standards had not yet arrived. Instead, the half-timer system, the simple straightforward ignoring of the law that said education was compulsory, and the excruciating boredom of much of school life, had all combined to ensure that there was variety in the numbers and ages of pupils in any given class. And, of course, to make quite certain that there were happy children who never, never went to school in their lives.

Having been placed in their new classes, the pupils had to be issued with their new school books. Mary helped the Master in this simple, if demanding, task. Every child had to have certain books. He also had to pay for them. Under the Master's direction, Mary handed out copy books and readers and history books and exercise books while the Master made out the account for each child. Most of the money would be brought in the following day, for all provident parents knew that school starting time was expensive, and had provided accordingly. Poor or improvident parents were given the benefit of a hire purchase system without interest, being thus enabled to pay off book bills at a penny or tuppence a week.

When Frederick came up for his new books, Mary was pleased and proud to have the necessary money to pay for his reader, history book, exercise book, jotter, pencil, ha'penny worth of nibs, pen-holder, Vere Foster copy book (one penny) and cover for same (one penny), incorporating two sheets of blotting paper. Little Sister, too, was provided for.

At the end of an easy but tiresome day, Mary and her charges made their way home, all with new books under their arms. Mary had particularly important books, for not only would she teach almost every day for the next forty-five years, but she would also have to study. Her apprenticeship would last five years, to be crowned with the coveted King's Scholarship. She worried a little about these books, for she had not had enough money for all. The Master had been very kind. He had insisted on lending her those she needed. She hoped she would be able to pay for them quickly.

As the three went down that beautiful road of theirs that looked as though it were a prepared avenue leading to some nobleman's estate, the sun was as brilliant as ever. The heat made Mary's dyed blacks sticky, and they smelled more of the dye than ever. She noticed that the damp of perspiration made the material smudge her skin. The other two ran on in front to the house to forage for immediate food and then to get out to their pets, the pretty pigeons, rabbits and hares. Mary moved more slowly up the side lane and round the back to the yard.

As she entered by the back door, she saw Aunt Laetitia dressed. Not that she ever was undressed. But there was a particular quality about her being dressed rather than just clothed. When she wore her rustling black silk, especially when she wore black velvet neck-ribbon with its cameo, you knew that Aunt Laetitia was dressed. You knew something was in the air. This was formality. Mary remembered. They were going to hear Pappy's Will. She felt guilty that with all the busy-ness and novelty and strain of the day she had forgotten to wonder about her loved Pappy's provision for them all.

Chapter 2

The hot, still evening drew on. Children, cattle and pets had all fed well. Now the two girls were busy carrying out Aunt Laetitia's directions in the dining room. Where their Aunt had placed the snowy cloth, they were setting out mother's best china, with its fine double lines of black and gold on white. They filled the cream ewer and sugar basin. They put out the thin rat-tailed spoons with the entwined initials of their paternal grand parents - N and J D. They set crystal boats of jam and glass dishes of butter. Mary had made the butter into small ridged rolls with the butter bats. The rolls glinted with drops of water as the evening sun shone, hot still, through the west facing bay window. Mary carefully pulled down the holland blinds to keep the table fresh. She shooed away a fly and was just in time to grab Little Sister's arm before it made a mighty smash with a book on a wasp hovering over a jam boat. When every hungry insect had been chased out into the hall, they closed the dining room door carefully. The rest of this peculiar meal - a kind of afternoon tea at night - would be prepared and served when the business of the law should be completed.

They crossed the hall together to the drawing room. Their Aunt had just given it the final dusting. The three boys came in from their outside chores. Lennox had some scarlet rambler roses in his hand and a spray of purple clematis. He loved flowers. He handed the brilliant posy to Mary. She exclaimed with delight and immediately wondered if such a bright offering of Nature would be considered suitable for this sad occasion. She was woefully ignorant of the etiquette of Will readings. Remembering Pappy's love of flowers, she took heart of grace and put them in water in an earthenware pot and brought it to the drawing room. Ever after, these flowers would remind her of the occasion.

'Clean and neat in their blacks, the five youngsters sat on the edges of drawing-room chairs.'

Clean and neat in their blacks, the five youngsters sat on the edges of drawing room chairs. Aunt Laetitia stood by the lace curtains at the window to catch the first glimpse of Mr Ferguson's pony and trap turning into their laneway. She was approaching sixty, but her tiny frame was upright and spare as ever. She turned and motioned to Alfred who sprang up gladly and rushed into the hall, out by the back door and round to the side gate of the yard. He stayed to stable and bait the pony while the two gentlemen went towards the back door to greet Aunt Laetitia. She led them through to the front hall where they hung their outer gear on the round pegs behind the door, and into the room of ceremony.

William John Ferguson had been Pappy's dearest friend. He was a tall youngish man, with handsome features and a carefully trimmed red beard, in shape resembling that of the new Prince of Wales. His was the pony and trap that had brought Mr Edward Hill from the Narrow Gauge Station in Doagh. Mr Hill, 'Ned' to his intimates, was the family solicitor. He was not nearly as tall as Mr Ferguson, but was a stocky, dark, kindly man with the red nose of the dyspeptic. He spoke very little but let the family friend introduce the topic of the evening.

Then Mr Hill read out the Will. Its legal jargon meant little to Mary. She realised that it said something to the effect that all Pappy's debts, if any, were to be paid first. Well, that seemed fair enough. It went on to say something about Aunt Laetitia having her day in the house, as she had come to look after his children. Well, thought Mary, that seems fair enough too. After all, she was almost sixty and it would hardly be right to turn her out now in her declining years.

In the meantime, the Will said to the children, they should try to find suitable careers if anything should happen to their Pappy, and on Aunt Laetitia's death everything would be sold and divided equally among his five children. That was that. It did not seem to Mary worth all the trouble they had taken to prepare a pretty tea table and get all dressed up. Alfred sat brooding in a corner. He kept his gaze fixed on the embroidered silk fire screen as though he could not see enough of it. As Aunt Laetitia, in her most gracious mood, conducted guests and children to supper, Alfred suddenly excused himself on the grounds of seeing that the pony was content. Everyone tucked in heartily to the scones and seed cake. Mr Hill had an extra cup of tea. All was relief and laughter.

Alfred slipped in and took a seat at the corner of the table. He wore a scowl. This meant nothing except that he was thinking. He was a devil-may-care, happy-go-lucky boy. Nevertheless, for the moment something had upset him. Mary stole glances at her eldest brother. Yes. He definitely was put out about something. Well, they would undoubtedly learn what it was in due time.

In the meantime, tea flowed. Frederick stock-piled carefully for a rainy day tomorrow. His first breakfast would consist of stale scone and dry seed cake. Little Sister sat on Mr Ferguson's knee as she used to sit on Pappy's. Pappy had called her his 'Little Love and Honour'. Now, her brown eyes smiled into Mr Ferguson's, as brown as hers. They were great friends. Aunt Laetitia chatted polite nothings to Mr Hill. Lennox made neat designs with the crumbs on his plate. No one but Mary took any notice of Alfred. He ate steadily, his eyes fixed on the table. He betrayed nothing to anyone. Something had happened to his world.

Next morning Mary awoke with a feeling of unease. For several minutes she couldn't place the cause. Then she noticed that something had happened to the usual morning sounds. Two stiff carts passed on the road. Mary jumped out of bed, her heart beating fast. Even as the blind flew up, she knew it was later than her usual waking time. She fairly pounced on Little Sister and shook her frantically. Mary was determined not to be late. If the others were late, that was their look-out. She washed and dressed, keeping up a string of scolds and threats until the child crawled out of bed. Mary seized her by the arm and dragged her to the wash basin. She pushed her head over the basin and held it there while she forcibly washed Little Sister's face. The child, bawled. Mary thrust a towel into her hand. She felt a glow of something uncannily like satisfaction. She ordered Little Sister into her clothes, and, buttoning her own blouse, flew down and up to the boys' landing. Nobody in Alfred's bed. Good. Lennox and Frederick fast asleep in theirs. Not so good. She soaked a face flannel in water and screwed it over the innocent sleeping faces. They awoke enraged, particularly Lennox who had a very quick temper. Mary flew downstairs. Heavens! After eight o'clock. Where on earth was Alfred? She rattled and banged at the range. The fire she set was so hurriedly laid that it promptly went out. She flung five bowls and spoons at the table. Very well. If they couldn't be up in time, they could go out like any working man on a bowl of porridge.

Where on earth was Alfred? From upstairs a rapid fire of coughs was all she got in reply. Pipe clearing was under way.

Mary ran into the pantry and filled a quart jug from the milk crock. This too was dumped on the table. Grimly she thought, 'Breakfast is served.'

Taking her bowl of porridge in one hand and her spoon in the other, she went to the bottom of the stairs and listened. Good. Everyone was certainly awake and moving. Supping porridge, she went to the back door. She found it unlocked. Alfred was up then. Of course he was up. He wasn't in bed, was he? She wandered round the yard, looking and supping. Then she stood still. Alfred was leaning on the gate to the water meadow. He was standing motionless looking towards the river.

After a moment's hesitation Mary called, 'Alfred, your breakfast's ready.' Having said it, she quickly amended it to, 'Alfred, your porridge's ready.' Still no reply. Not a move. What on earth was wrong with him? She essayed the small voice. 'Alfred, the fire's out.' The boy was still. He did not turn to her. Mary's temper was as quick as Lennox's. She flung around and went indoors without another word. She just had to get herself and the others out in time. In time? They were already late. Never was porridge eaten so fast nor lunches put up more quickly. If they ran they would be in good enough time. Alfred still stood by the gate, leaning on its friendly bars. Mary was not to know it for weeks, but at that moment Alfred was saying good-bye to his homeland. For the first time in his life, he was feeling the touch of bitterness. He was the eldest son, but the law of primogeniture was not to apply to him, it seemed. One of his emotions on hearing Pappy's Will had been that of humiliation. This was not to be soothed until five years later when he would make a brilliant return to the little County Antrim farm from far-off Wyoming, wearing stetson and chaps, and speaking with a new voice. A real cowboy from the other world of the Wild West.

Mary and the two small ones hurried up the road. Alternately, they ran and trotted. When they overtook the first children moving towards school, Mary made the others slow with her to a sedate walk. They were in quite good time after all. Nothing was going to interfere with her budding dignity as a child-teacher. This time she walked into the school porch, leaving her brother and sister in the yard. She looked round the porch, wondering which way to go.

To outward view, this school was two storeys high. In previous times this had been so, when the school mistress and her husband, the mill cashier, had lived in an apartment below the upper storey school. Before Mary's day, this intervening ceiling-floor had been removed and the Big Room was high and airy. It still sported the upstairs and downstairs rows of windows of former days, so that it was well lighted.

The intervening floor had been removed when the next teacher, Miss Henry, followed the cashier and his school ma'am wife. Miss Henry lived in the first of the row of cottages joined on to the large single school room. After Miss Henry came Miss Barr and Miss Picken who did not live at the school at all. Instead, Miss Henry's cottage was taken over to provide a class-room for the second teacher. A hallway with pegs for coats separated the two classrooms.

The Cogry Mills continued to grow and prosper. The population grew with it. A piece was chopped off the scutch mill adjoining the school house on the other side. This sizeable portion was separated from the Big Room by the porch where Mary stood. The scutch classroom was called the Big Gallery, the cottage classroom was the Low Gallery. Mary never knew why it was not called the Wee Gallery which would have been more appropriate, but 'wee' was an Ulsterism not encouraged by the pedagogues, while 'little' came awkwardly to the Ulster tongue. At any rate, the school now consisted of three class-rooms separated by two porches or hallways.

Mary knocked timidly on the door into the Big Room. It was the likely place to find the Master, she reckoned. No reply from the silent door. She knocked again more loudly than she had intended. 'Come in,' said the Master. Mary went in.

John Parkinson McNally was a young man with a passion for both cleanliness and Godliness. His dark Mediterranean face was surmounted by a sleek cap of black hair, and adorned with a small, black, military moustache. About him there was a faint aura as of a Regimental Sergeant-Major manqué. He was impeccable in his dress - neatly brushed and pressed navy-blue serge, showing snowy linen cuffs and high white collar. He drove a glittering trap and cream coloured pony as neat and well turned out as himself. He could not abide dirty children.

Each morning, every pupil presented hands and face for his inspection - in dubious cases, necks and ears, and bare feet and legs also. The unfortunates who did not pass the inspection were lined up. The leader was handed a bucket of soft soap, a gift from the mill, and a towel. The line about-turned and headed for the river bank and a perilous climb to the river below. Even in the depths of winter, these children had to remove the cause

'About him there was a faint aura as of a Regimental Sergeant-Major manqué.'

of offence. The soap and towel were passed along the line of culprits until all had at least the appearance of cleanliness. The towel was sodden when it reached the last child. The river provided the towel itself with a final rinse. This sopping cloth was spread on the Big Room fire guard to dry for the dirty children of the morrow. To Mary it was a puzzle to decide where cleanliness began and hygiene ended!

The Master was a hard man. He drove everyone with little mercy. He drove himself with even less. His mainsprings of interest were his interpretation of Christ Crucified and his genuine love of music. To Mary he often showed kindness. Yet he found no difficulty in reconciling the love of God with soaking a bucketful of canes in cold water on Friday, ready for the slaughter of the innocents, dirty or stupid or both, on the coming Monday.

Swish! Swish! Swish! went the wet canes on trembling bony fingers thrust out with pale faced bravado. The water droplets flew in the sunshine in iridescent replicas of the promise of God's eternal love.

'Shall we gather at the River,' sang the Master lustily the same afternoon.

'Where bright angels' feet have trod.
With its crystal tide forever
Flowing by the Throne of God?
Yes, we will gather at the River

(firmly, for the Master was certain of himself, if dubious of others)

The beautiful, the beautiful, the River,
Gather with the saints at the River
Flowing by the Throne of God.'

Mary had one of her old giggles at the thought of slightly dubious angels lining up at the River Beautiful, with soft soap and sodden heavenly towel, making quite sure, under the Master's eye, that their feet were of the requisite brightness.

In the Big Room, the Master told Mary that she would start her teaching career with an Infant Class in the Big Gallery. She went there to await the first challenge. The Master exited with his hand bell to line up his charges on the cassie, class by class, all marking time with shod or bare feet on the cinders. Mary's Infants marched into the Big Gallery, filling each tier of the room that was built up just like 'the gods' of a theatre. Angelic eyes, row upon row, stared at her, shrewdly sizing her up. 'There's the wall chart,' said the Master. 'And there's the pointer.' He went out and shut the door. The angelic eyes swivelled to the door and back to Mary. There was an almost imperceptible shimmer of movement, of sound.

Mary faced her very first class resolutely. She handed the pointer to a curly haired clean face in the front row. 'Now, you come out and read, Charlie,' she said with firm voice and trembling knees. She didn't know whether this was a new lesson on the wall chart or an old one. She only knew it was going to be *the* one.

She found with faint surprise and some relief that Charlie came out as requested. Pointer in hand, he hazarded the first faltering words of the lesson on the chart. Mary prompted him when his resolution or academic resources failed. Charlie struggled gamely through to the end. 'Now you, Henry,' said Mary.

Henry scrambled with alacrity out of the third tier. Waving the pointer nonchalantly at any section, he gabbled the lesson from beginning to end non-stop. Mary felt that on her first day she must become mistress of this and every other situation.

'Right, Henry,' she said bravely. 'Now close your eyes and "read" it to me again.'

Grinning with pride, Henry closed his eyes and repeated the lesson. Mary had learnt a lesson too.

'Open your eyes,' said she, 'and tell me what that word is? No? - That one? - No? - That one?'

There was no sound. Henry was very young and crimson. He still tried to grin, although there was a glitter about his eyes.

'It's all right, Henry,' said the new teacher. 'Now we'll find out the words together.'

Mary's teaching career was launched.

On the night after Pappy's Will was read, all five youngsters met by arrangement round the kitchen range. Chores were done. On the other side of the hatch, Aunt Laetitia was safely ensconced in the dining room. By the light of the setting sun, she was completing the melancholy task of answering letters of condolence. With their Aunt absent, the children could talk confidentially together and try to make something like plans for the future.

As a first step, Lennox refused point blank to go back to school for any more 'business training.' He hated it. School was awful, horrible, dreadful. He was no good at the subjects. Except book keeping! Lennox could always look after money, and had cash in hand when everyone else in the house was penniless. He lent out shillings and pennies to those in want and called in his loans when he needed money himself. Thus he was able to call in one hundred pounds to add to Aunt Laetitia's twenty when he later left home. But it must be said of him that he never put out his money upon usury!

At this particular moment, however, a thin schoolboy of sixteen, he was on strike. No more school. Not ever. He poked the low fire in the kitchen range, sat back, folded his arms and defied anyone to budge him. Mary felt hopeless. What on earth could she do with him? And he was her favourite.

Of all the family, she herself was the only one working to earn money. Well, she hadn't actually got any of it yet, but Monitresses were paid while learning their trade. For this, her first year, Mary would receive five pounds, payable in quarterly instalments of twenty five shillings. Not a fortune, but nevertheless a help. No one could pretend that it was enough to support even herself. Nonetheless, of them all, her future was the most assured, and this fact made her feel responsible for the others.

They all turned to Frederick's plight. Soon he would reach the statutory leaving age and his schooling would have to end. They would 'look around' for something useful and profitable for him to do. But what? They gave up the conundrum temporarily. Frederick relaxed. 'Sufficient unto the day,' he meditated, and thoughtfully chewed a left over sandwich. Mary felt disappointed about him. Pappy had made such a fetish of everyone's having that extra schooling, those years in which to prepare to face the world. Yet here sat his brood of five staring an inimical world in the face, so many little Davids with naught but the tiniest of pebbles for their particular Goliaths.

Mary realised sorrowfully that, while Pappy had been dear and handsome and loving, he was no businessman. How *could* there be so little money now? With the others, she took stock. Lennox made out careful notes. Alfred said nothing but looked on with a tolerant if sardonic eye. Little Sister, from her stool, looked up at them all with trusting brown eyes.

First, there were two farmhouses and two farms. Then there were the labourers' cottages at the foot of the lane. There were Granpa James's rows of little houses in the working class areas of Belfast. There was all the goodwill of Pappy's business ventures. There were even people who owed Pappy money.

One of the first great lessons the children learned before they issued forth into the great world at all was that, if a man owed you money, he did not necessarily pay you - even if, or perhaps even because, you were a child and an orphan. It was a hard, cruel lesson, but from it emerged a little shining truth. For there

27

was one man, one righteous man, who came every week to the back door of the Bridge House with a careful shilling or a florin from his meagre pay until his debt to the dead was fully repaid. He too had five children. Mary never forgot to respect him - nor, indeed, to despise those who took advantage of five orphans and an old woman.

But facts must be faced. Pappy had just no idea when he made his Will that he had left everything so tied up and tangled that after his business debts were sorted out and paid - and it took one farmhouse with its good fields to do that - there was only the unearned income from letting some rather small, rather old houses, and from letting the Bridge House land at ten pounds a year. And Aunt Laetitia must be maintained first and foremost.

This last sum - ten pounds a year - seemed even to Mary to be a very small sum. It was a strange arrangement. But surely it must be all right? They all sat and stared at the last embers of the fire. Ten pounds. And the little rents. And Aunt Laetitia to keep. Could it be done? Well, it had to be done. So it was done.

Chapter 3

The spring of the year nineteen hundred and four came late. In March, the trees and hedgerows had as yet no hesitant gauze of green nor gloss of sticky buds. In this chill season, while the tiny snowdrops still clung to life in frosty winds, a tiny child, as fine and delicate as the pale flowers, came to the Bridge House.

She was just past her second birthday, and for such a very small person, had a compensatingly long name - Martha Jane Stevenson Dugan. This name was altogether too much for her, and she herself shortened it to an amusing and memorable 'Moxie' and Moxie she ever after remained.

When she arrived by train from Derry, she was 'Poor Cousin Harry's' baby. 'Poor Cousin Harry' was so called because he had been bereft of his wife by Moxie's birth. The nursemaid he had procured for the motherless baby and her older brother and sister, had proved not only unreliable but positively dangerous, it being discovered that she was much addicted to the use of laudanum for silencing crying children.

The family rallied as usual to combat a common menace. The baby's brother was sent to stay with his mother's sister, Aunt Airlie. The baby's sister went to her mother's other sister, Auntie Frances. Only the baby came to her father's cousins.

Little Moxie was a sad baby with dark-set eyes and fine, lank hair. She arrived wearing a Red Riding Hood cape of warm flannel which covered her from head to toe and nearly overwhelmed her tiny face. Cousin Harry's Aunt had brought her by train from Derry.

This Aunt was a very great personage indeed. She was never addressed any more familiarly than as 'Miss Ada.' She was the headmistress of Derry Model Infants' School, and was a woman of large and commanding presence and great mental gifts. As if all this were not enough, she had written a nationally used text book on mathematics, and composed a brilliant mnemonic rhyme to aid students of history to wend their way date-wise from ten-sixty-six onwards. Still unexhausted, she had put pen to paper to create what was probably the first map of the world showing the products, commerce and industry of its regions as well as their political boundaries. Not even yet was her genius diminished, for she set to and invented a patent spring bed for invalids. Altogether she was a most fearsome, witty and infinitely kind woman.

Miss Ada was Moxie's great aunt and Aunt Laetitia's cousin. Over the Bridge House tea table, the two elderly ladies decided the baby's future.

'About what age do you think? Some more seed cake?' Aunt Laetitia pressed politely.

'Thank you, no,' said Miss Ada declining. 'Oh, about seven, I should think. Or eight. No, I expect about seven would do.'

The baby staggered round the dining room table, reaching up small determined hands to pull at the damask cloth. Mary put her hand firmly on the cloth to hold it. The baby sat down on the floor. After deliberating for a few seconds, she got up again and went staggering on her long journey round the table.

'Just so long as she can do up her own buttons and tapes,' said Miss Ada in her firm, kind voice. 'From then on, I can see to her future.'

'I think that could be managed,' said Aunt Laetitia. 'Yes, until she's about seven. Yes, I can manage.'

Like so many courageous Victorians, she assumed near impossible tasks out of a sense of duty, and brought them to successful conclusions. Had she not already brought poor dead William's children to near adulthood, and she a maiden lady of sixty years?

'Then she shall come to me at Crawford Square,' asserted Miss Ada. 'I know nothing really of caring for babies so young, but - just old enough to do up her own clothes, you know. From then on, I shall be able to provide all she needs. And she must have a first class education. Most important, that is. Most important. And eventually she shall have all I possess. That should take care of her. Poor baby.'

Long before she could do up her buttons, the pale little baby had lost her Miss Ada, whose sudden death shocked the family even more than had that of the late Queen. And little Moxie was to be the Bridge House children's playmate and friend for all the rest of her life. They were to be her family and her home. 'Poor Cousin Harry' decided to try his luck in Canada and went, taking the baby's brother, Cyril, with him. Little May remained with the Stevenson aunts, little Moxie with her father's cousins. She was *their* baby.

And though, later, her Stevenson aunts would offer her the inducement of much more of this world's goods than Aunt Laetitia ever could provide, she stayed loyally with those who were the first and only loving family she could remember.

And after all the chat and the seed cake, it turned out that Miss Ada, engrossed in books, beds and bursaries, had, in fact, forgotten to make a Will at all!

The spring that brought Moxie to the Bridge House took Alfred away from it. He was now a tall, thin, dark haired young man of twenty. He had a merry, roving disposition, and his mother's brown eyes that could laugh so easily.

He was in a fever to be off as the time for emigration drew nearer and nearer. The family took it all rather matter-of-factly, for, truth to tell, they did not realise the full implications of emigrating to America.

Alfred would go away, Alfred would come back. Between these two events, he would have marvellous adventures and carry out Aunt Laetitia's strong injunction to seek his fortune. She was the only person Mary had ever heard using these actual words. They were a measure of Aunt Laetitia's grasp of the true situation, for she sent the youth across the Atlantic with a one way ticket and twenty pounds in his pocket.

That he survived, and moreover survived to return with a little more money in his pocket, proved only the existence of that great and merciful Providence that watched over at least some orphans of bygone days.

Alfred was one of the gayest people Mary ever knew, although he could draw his dark eyebrows down in a scowl that momentarily robbed his face of its good looks. When he was not immersed in books, his laughter was infectious, his sense of humour zany as a clown's, and his immense love of practical jokes a sure recipe for unpopularity with the pompous and the proud.

And he himself was not too proud to display his jesting habits to even friendly neighbours. As, for example, to old Grannie and Granda Mellon, a delightful ancient couple who lived up the Thorn Dyke loney.

There was a short cut from the Bridge House to the Thorn Dyke through the fields. One day Alfred had to deliver a skittish young lady pig to Mellon's farmyard. He set off whistling, driv-

'*Alfred delivered himself of an airy exposition on his piggy-back ride all the way from Bridge House.*'

ing the sow before him, up by Jane Kirk's where the massed sweet lilacs grew, and across the fields and by the Granny's Knowes to the Thorn Dyke.

As he approached the long whitewashed farmhouse, he caught a glimpse of Granda Mellon at work in the yard. Quick as a flash, Alfred threw one long leg over the pig's back and 'rode' his unusual steed round the corner and into the yard.

The old man stood at gaze for several minutes, eyes and mouth open. Alfred languidly 'dismounted,' and delivered himself of an airy exposition on his piggy back ride all the way from Bridge House. The Mellons, good souls, believed that story till their dying day. They didn't know their Alfred.

Alfred left home on an evening in late spring. Twilight had descended before he was dressed and ready to leave for the Upper Station and the train to Derry. They had decided, Alfred most firmly of all, that there would be no public farewells at the quay side or the station. He would say a nonchalant cheerio at his own back door and walk off into the spring night.

Mary was grateful, for she felt that she could not bear it if she had to watch a train carrying him away into the distance, or a ship slowly moving out into Lough Foyle towards the broad Atlantic. Alfred going out by the back door was just Alfred going out by the back door. And as usual he would come in again by it. In time.

His cabin trunk, that had been Pappy's for his journeyings in America, was already sent on ahead. Alfred looked as though he were travelling very light indeed. Dressed in his good suit, his heavy coat over his arm, sandwiches in one pocket, books, paper and pencils in all other pockets, he pushed his newly acquired black bowler hat rakishly so that it sat on the back of his head. He grinned his usual sardonic smile, gave them all a mock salute. The door closed behind him.

Alfred was gone. Tall, thin, dark, lovely, funny Alfred was gone. Gone to meet his friend Bob Ferguson and with him cross the thousands of miles to his Promised Land. Gone and left a sad and somehow guilty void behind. All that night, Mary wept for another part of her life that was gone with him.

The Christmas of 1904 was not the first at which the children had felt a loss. Nine years earlier, they had their first Christmas without mother. One year earlier, their first Christmas without Pappy. Now Christmas would come and there would be no Alfred.

But that blessed baby would make up for a lot. Mary and Little Sister decided to do something they had never done before. They decided to go out and spend precious money on a Christmas gift, a present for little Moxie.

Mary had a certain financial independence now. With twenty-five shillings, her very first salary, at the end of September of the previous year she had gone to Belfast with Aunt Laetitia and bought herself her very first independently owned garment - a coat. It was a wonderful and exciting experience. The coat of black and white flecked Donegal tweed with deep cuffs, collar and revers of neat black bainin, took all of her quarter's salary, but was very well worth it, for it lasted for years upon years, and, as her old friend Beenie, once maid-of-all-work at the Bridge, told her, it always 'looked the money'!

In her second year, Mary's annual pay went up from £5 to £6 - thirty shillings every quarter. Most of this went straight to Aunt Laetitia to help keep family heads above water, but Mary determinedly hung on to sixpence from her September salary. It was destined for baby Moxie.

In Ballyclare there was one of the most wonderful shops in all the world - Fanny Cannon's. It was on the left as one pro-ceeded down the Main Street, a toy shop joined to its house in which Fanny lived. From her front room as she sat crocheting, Fanny, a tall, iron grey woman, could see into her shop through a glazed door. To serve, she merely had to lay down her work, push her spectacles to the top of her head and step into the shop. On Christmas Eve, 1904, Mary and Little Sister clasped one another's hands as they jostled and shoved their way through the crowds of Christmas shoppers on the pavement of Main Street. Light and dark were intermittent in the early evening, as one moved from shop window to shop window. It was said that the new Urban Council, only two months old, was going to provide street lighting with oil lamps just as good as in any great city. In the meantime, light was fitful from the lamp of one gay window to the next.

Moving candle-lights on the muddy street showed the dark moving shapes of horse traps and pony traps, the sidecars and the huge black swaying boxes of the bakers' vans. Swinging hurricane lamps hung from the trambs of stiff carts. The girls had to be on the look out for cars and carts left on the pavement edge, shafts in the air, their horses gone to the livery stables and their owners to the shops. An occasional brilliant white light piercing the darkness came from the still rare bicycle. No light at all illumined the infrequent horseman.

'Moving candle-lights on the muddy street showed the dark
moving shapes of horse-traps and pony-traps.'

Bicycles touched Mary's heart dearly. She had wanted a bicycle for as long as she could remember. She had almost lost her reputation for having even a modicum of sense because of a bicycle. It was Pappy's bicycle, a bone shaker with narrow tyres of solid red rubber, for that Belfastman, John Dunlop, had brought forth his new-fangled pneumatic tyre only in the year of Mary's birth. The solid tyre was still *de rigueur* around Doagh.

To ride Pappy's bicycle at all - and for the learner it was an advantage - one had first to wheel the conveyance to the head of the gently sloping Big Field. Safely mounted, the rider could steer the bumping brute all the way down the field, on to the back lane still on a slight incline, and then take a sharp turn at the lane's foot on to the county road, mercifully free of traffic. All the while, one had to pedal. There were no brakes, bells, lights or any such unnecessary refinements.

One hot summer's day, Mary had donned her bathing costume, a precious luxury for holidays at Pappy's old home at Castlerock. The costume of long drawers and tunic top was in heavy blue and white ticking with a sailor collar, and elegant frills at cuffs and calves. On her head she wore Alfred's straw hat. Into the shimmering heat of a June afternoon she surreptitiously wheeled the bicycle. The house was somnolent. Up the Big Field she went, panting and sweating slightly in spite of the unaccustomed freedom of her clothes. She gave the bicycle a good push off, flew down the Big Field pedalling furiously, gathering momentum all the time, down the lane, into the roadway, still pedalling, and steered gently into the summer hedgerow. Time after time, she repeated the joyous laborious feat. The last time, she looked up from the hedgerow of perfumed hawthorn and blue violets into the pink and white face of the Rector. His pale eyes bulged in his head. Like the late Queen, he was not amused. He was, however, discreet. Not a word reached the family's ears.

A high cold wind blew from the icy North. It whistled round corners and blew gentlemen's hats into the rough, rutted street. It positively shrieked by the time the two girls reached Fanny Cannon's. They were glad to push open the glazed door with its clanging bell, and step into the exciting crowded haven of the Toy Emporium.

All that day they had been busy preparing for Christmas Day on the morrow. The pudding, now rather an annual than a daily affair, had boiled for hours suspended in its floured cloth in the steaming black oval pot. The raisins and muscatels plumpened and grew lush in the sugary heat. The spicy odours of Christmas hung in the air. A rather elderly Rhode Island Red, well past the lay, had departed this life and turned into a chicken instead. Slowly parboiled, then stuffed and roasted, she would provide good Christmas fare, with choice of turnip or drumhead from the fields and fine floury potatoes. Now the present for their own baby would set the seal on a busy, happy day.

The girls stared excitedly at Fanny's counter which ran round three sides of her shop. On shelves, on counters, from ceiling, on floor, in every conceivable and some nearly inconceivable places were toys and playthings for children. There were dolls of china and dolls of wax, rag dolls, and baby dolls. Wicker cradles and wicker prams for all dolls. Tin tea sets for rag dolls and china tea sets for upper class dolls. Dolls' houses with the windows and doors merely painted on. Other dolls' houses whose whole roofs came off, showing every room and every inhabitant and furnishing to the last detail. There were hoops, drums, trumpets, penny whistles, peeries, marlies, pops, flags, cocked hats, swords, tin soldiers, bats, balls, whips and tops, toy trains, dogs, Noah's Arks, Jack-in-the-boxes, clock alphabets for ambitious children, humming tops for light-headed children, paint boxes for artistic children - there was just everything you could name. And then all those you had forgotten. Like slates and pencils, fishing nets, building blocks, souvenirs that said 'A Present from Ballyclare,' golden singing birds, that filled with water, piped and trilled in the blower's breath, Snap cards, books of nursery rhymes, dominoes, bagatelle, checkaboord (draughts) - the piled up wealth upon wealth of childish joy that stretched to infinity.

Mary and Little Sister wandered through this Aladdin's Cave, fingering and wondering, considering and rejecting. At last the final, the inevitable, choice was made. On one of the counters just within Little Sister's reach was a donkey. He was grey and amiable. Little Sister stretched out a hand to pat him. His head nodded back to her. They both shouted with pleasure and touched him again. Again he nid-nodded to their touch. The girls looked at one another and then at Fanny's face 'How much?' they wondered. Mary clutched the hot sixpence in her pocket. From the slight, kind smile on Fanny's face she could read nothing.

'How much?' she said at last.

'Sixpence,' said Fanny.

Mary almost fainted with relief. The donkey was so perfect, so right. With pleasure she handed over the silver, and Fanny wrapped the donkey in a large sheet of brown paper and tied him up with string. The two girls smiled at each other in that pure joy which is the joy of the giver.

'Here, you carry it,' Mary handed the purchase to Little Sister. They would share the pleasure of carrying it home.

Once more in the busy, blown street, they turned to go up by the Market Square again and home by the Doagh Road. The wind shrieked more and more loudly. Mary was glad of her warm coat. She took the parcel back from her young sister and, hand in hand, they started battling against the wind that now swirled round corners and attacked them icily from unexpected angles. At times, it was so strong that they could have leaned hard against it without falling. Twigs and left over leaves from autumn hit them smart little taps on their cold red faces. They struggled the two and a half miles home to Bridge House, clutching jelly bag caps and the precious, wonderful donkey.

Never, thought Mary, had she been so glad to turn into their own lane and run round by the farm yard to the back door. They almost fell into the back hall. The shrieking in the house stopped as they banged the door shut.

'Look,' shouted Little Sister joyfully to the others in the kitchen lamplight. Baby Moxie was safely in bed.

'Look what we got.'

In the spicy, steamy kitchen, Aunt Laetitia, Lennox and Frederick stared in stupefaction. What was held out with proud excited delight to their gaze was an empty, crumpled piece of paper, and some string.

Chapter 4

Long, long ago, when Ballyclare was but a bridging place on the Six-Mile-Water - a rude village of nomadic herdsmen - the inhabitants took an annual jaunt to the hill grazing above the valley. This left behind two interesting sociological remnants, the May Fair and the Lammas Fair. Cattle that had been successfully over wintered by the river were sold at the great Fair in May. Those which had been taken to the grassy uplands to reach full fatness in summer were brought down to be sold at the Lammas Fair in the Fall.

Both Fairs took place on a hillside sloping towards the river - the Fair Hill. The important huts, inns and trading places arose in the area of this Fair Hill, and alongside the path running down to the river. This path became, in time, Main Street. The Fair Hill became (by grace of that great land owner, the Marquess of Donegall) the Market Square, still on such a brisk slope as to cause a considerate carter to walk his horse.

As well as the two great annual Fairs, Ballyclare had weekly markets, every Monday and Tuesday. In nineteen hundred and four, the Market House stood, firm and uncompromising, in the Market Square. Downstairs was the Market House proper. Upstairs was a large room which provided a social centre for local traders and farmers and minor gentry, and offered a local habitation for balls and soirees, bazaars and concerts. In this large room, Mary suffered the greatest humiliation of her life at a concert when she and one of her friends, a pleasant boy called Fred McNally, (youngest brother of the Master), were to play a pianoforte duet - 'The Band on the Pier.' Fred was willing and anxious to get started. Mary ceased to realise that there were people in the hall, even that there were notes on the page in front of her. She became oblivious of her audience. In fact, she became oblivious of everything. She had gone blank. The candles in their brass holders shone serenely on piano and music sheets. Several times Fred ventured his introductory notes. Mary still stared like a stuck pig. After an agonised few minutes, Fred gathered up 'The Band on the Pier,' and Mary retired with him, crimson with self-conscious shame. Thus Mary's public musical career came to an end without a blow, or even a note, being struck.

Davy Cameron the printer, whose shop had the Market House under its eye, took care of the building. His neighbour, Tom McKnight the tailor, played a second role as Weigh Master. As each stiff-cart lurched towards the great square of iron on the floor that was the weighbridge, Tom's constant call rang out, 'Mine the kerbstane! How money hae ye got?'

Ranged round inside the Market House were the stalls of local and itinerant merchants, and of farmers selling their wares - brown eggs and white eggs, lumps, pats, tubs and firkins of country butter, live chickens, buttermilk in runlets and sweet milk in large cans of thick tin, cheese, honey, souvenirs and fancy goods and webs of materials from all over the world that had now supplanted the homespun and brown linen of earlier times.

On one side of Davy's shop was the fruit shop of John Morrison - 'Scallion Jock' to one and all. To the north side, Tom was flanked by West's boot store and School Street. On the further corner of School Street was the charming home of Mary's medical adviser, Dr Stevenson. In turn followed Wilson the Saddler, Erskine the Milliner and Lawson the Draper, so that one came thus to the fine new Northern Bank. Outside the bank was a huge tree, waving branches of welcome shade that were soon to be brought low in a Big Wind, nearly taking Mary's life with them in their mighty fall. On the north side of the Square were Miss Boyd's grocery store, N B Warwick's paper shop, Shannon's handsome Emporium, and, in a sticking out kind of house - that was to be removed seventy years later to facilitate traffic - the offices of the local auctioneers, Craig and McClelland.

The most interesting building on the east side of the Square was undoubtedly that first supermarket of Ireland, James Gregg's shop. This last simple little word can give no idea of the business that thronged this merchant's premises. Downstairs he was a druggist, a grocer, a hardware merchant, a meal, flour and seedsman, and right at the back of the long, long shop, a publican with a busy bar. Upstairs, the billiard hall! Over the way, the hairdressing establishment! And, presiding over everything, the huge white cockatoo that urged all customers in passing to 'Scratch Cocky! Scratch Cocky!'

James Gregg was a benevolent and wealthy white bearded patriarch. Liza Jane, his sister, kept a shrewd eye to business, while his son, Sam, trained himself to follow carefully in his father's footsteps.

But James' daughter, an heiress, and more than a little haughty, was always 'Miss Elizabeth' in the style of Jane Austen, or 'Miss Lizzy' to her more intimate acquaintances.

North of James Gregg's magnificent place of business came - very naturally somewhat lower in stature - the Ulster Bank; next, the house of the visiting dentist; next, the claustrophobic, dark and exciting shop of the druggist, Johnny McConnell; and finally, the little old Ballyclare National School, with its outside staircase to the Upper Room that had been the school house and its downstairs that was the Master's abode.

The little street that ran down by the side of Gregg's shop connected the daily life of the front town to that of its one back street, rather grandly called Park Street. Here one found the doss houses of old Mrs McDonald, of the dummy's mother, Mrs McGaw, and of Rosie Craig who also ran a rag store to provide material for the best paper in the Ballyclare paper mills. Alex Graham, the butcher, sold fine meat here, and many local grandees visited the fruit shop of Andy Phillips, a good businessman with bad feet and a bad temper. Here, too, lived Jinny McClean, female sexton of the Covenanters' Church, with her eighteen cats.

Ballyclare was famous for its number of churches of all denominations. These were outnumbered only by its pubs - Gregg's, Frank Baird's at the foot of the town, 'Shines' Services (sparkling with cleanliness), Robert Baird's (the Ollardale Hotel, with gardens famous for miles around), McTier's Bar, John Grange's, the Other Grange's up in the Square, Henry Service's (the only spirit grocery), Sam Kissock's and Houston Craig's one-storeyed thatched cottage pub in the middle of Main Street.

As for churches, there was the Catholic Church on the Doagh Road, with Annie Docherty as its sexton. Annie lived in McClean's Entry and was famous for wearing her boots only on Sunday in order to show proper respect for the Holy Day. On week days, she ran back and forth to her work of cleaning and polishing, with bare feet hardened on the stony streets. In the same month as Mary started her career, Father O'Boyle started a fund to build a new church. That quiet man and Protestant Christian, Ned Hill, gave the site to Ballyclare's Catholics just across the road from their old church that had been in use since 1832, and the stone-masons, whose work in the Church of the

Sacred Heart is still a monument to their craftsmanship, were these two stout Orangemen, Sam McClean and Sam Bell, perhaps the two most prominent and certainly among the most respected Protestants in the town.

Then there were the Old Presbyterians in Main Street (somehow or other mixed up at times and called Unitarians) who had the oldest church. It had been established in 1652, only eleven short years after the terrible Rising of 1641.

Their offshoot New Presbyterians had a fine church on the Doagh Road, whilst the Church of Ireland had not yet risen to the proud honour of a proper church building. They had a tin hut. This was rather an odd state of affairs, as they had in their joint parishes of Ballynure and Ballyeaston two fine dressed-stone buildings. It seemed to Mary very curious indeed to see Ballyeaston's handsome church de-roofed and left to rot, while two miles away the same parishoners worshipped under corrugated iron. As Ballyeaston had two flourishing Presbyterian Churches, she decided as a child that *her* Church had been ruined by some deep Presbyterian plot, and it took her years to get over this childish impression.

The Reformed Presbyterians were always called the 'Covenanters', who also went in for the corrugated style of architecture on the Ballycorr Road. Above Scallion Jock's was the Protestant Hall where the Orangemen met, and which was to become the Salvation Army Citadel when the Orangemen finally got a hall of their own.

Ballyclare had a long and well respected Methodist tradition, the Wesleyans worshipping in their square grey church by the Bridge over the Six-Mile River.

In the ecclesiastically styled building that was to become the Technical School the Congregationalists worshipped, always suffering under the stiff-necked nickname of the 'Independents.' Later, when Mary went to cookery classes there, she did so under the benign Gothic windows the Independents had left as their memorial.

And they dared to say of such a town:

'Sweet Ballyclare where they keep no Sunday,
And every day's like an Easter Monday.'

Added to these more or less orthodox sects were innumerable halls for Evangelicals, Brethren, Cooneyites, Holy Rollers, visiting Faith Missioners, and all who were out for a lively rousing bit of religious cleansing, for this was the great and glorious hey-day of Moody and Sankey, while the shadow of the great Nicholson,

42

and even of Charles Spurgeon, still fell darkly across the minds and hearts of sinners.

In the yard by Willie Lard-Hips' pork butchery was the secret and awful room where the Exclusive Brethren worshipped, in the same place where Miss Aicken's Ladies' School was later established.

Of all these sectarian worshippers, there was little doubt that the Mission Halls had the best of it, with joyous music and lurid sermons, with endless opportunities of hearing aloud the colour-ful sins of others, and with plenty of pranks on the way home. On second thoughts, the Salvation Army probably ran neck and neck to the winning post (if they will forgive such an expression) with joy, joy, joy and a lot of sense and stability forbye!

Yet, in all his forays into the religious life, the Ulsterman seldom lost completely his pawky sense of humour. Once Mary, a stout Episcopalian, was drawn out of curiosity to hear the great Nicholson himself. Nothing remains of his harangue, but the incident is crystal clear of a man who, bored, busy or guilty, got up early to leave the meeting.

'Behold that man!' thundered Nicholson. 'Behold him, brethren, heading straight for hell!'

Provoked, the man turned.

'I'll let your granny know you're comin'!' he shouted and slammed the door.

The Cunningham brothers ran their Blue House in simple emulation of James Gregg. In their establishment, one bought not only drapery and haberdashery, but linoleum, furniture, Bibles and prayer books, wallpaper, boots and shoes and fine brass stair rods. Beside the Blue House was Williamson the jeweller, who would go on to the end of his life putting up the black shutters to protect his goods, just as he did now in 1904. Then came the new chemist, Mr Calvert. Next, jutting out some yards, was the new Post Office.

Beside Mrs Armstrong's Post Office lived the postman, Andy Nesbitt, who conducted a thriving business in his little shop selling broadsheets, song sheets, poems, melodeons, penny whistles, french fiddles and Jew's harps. Andy's shop was followed by those of Doran the barber and Mick Griffin the butcher. Here, too, one found the upstairs office of the Bridge children's solicitor, Mr Edward Hill, beside McConnell's large posting establishment, and so to Robert McCrea's.

Robert was the coal merchant, with his good standby the weighbridge beside the Narrow Gauge Railway Station. Before one took the inclined path down from the Main Street to the Booking Office, one passed the loaded stiff carts waiting to be weighed. They were full of coal brought in the Narrow Gauge train wagons from Larne. Robert shoved each stiff cart on to the iron weighbridge, loosed the horse's bellyband, and propped a little stick under the trambs so that only the cart and coal were weighed. Having weighed the empty cart as it passed him on its way to the train, he could work out weight and price in fantastically rapid mental arithmetic that was never wrong.

Those who came in from the country on Market days or on Saturday afternoons after work had finished at half past twelve could count on a number of diversions. Apart from the many pubs - never visited by women, with the exception of Henry Service's Spirit Grocery, where twopence worth of porter could be carried out in a can covered by a shawl - there were the 'atin' houses' providing food. These ranged from the Central Dining Rooms where a decent farmer could get his legs under a table with a cloth on it for the better enjoyment of a good dinner, to shops for the sale of chips and fish or that great snack of the age - hot peas. Bella Price in Main Street provided not only hot peas but hot broth on Market days, and kept lodgers. Mrs Carlin on the other hand kept lodgers, but, a rung or two on the social ladder above hot peas, sold groceries at the foot of the town.

If a man wanted neither food nor drink, he might have his hair, beard and moustache trimmed at Simms', Doran's or Esler's. Or he might go for a fitting to any of the six tailors who, cross-legged, sat sewing busily in their shops to make every suit bespoke - John Forsythe, Willie Lorimer, Tom McKnight, Davie Hill, Jim Boyd or John Graham.

His wife had an enviable number of drapers to call on, although the milliners too had a busy time, in an age when each hat could be fitted, blocked, made up, and trimmed by hand to the customer's requirements. The finest milliner was Miss McIlroy in the first shop below the Bridge by the Methodist Church. Here, if money could not be spared for a new hat, last year's model could be stripped to its bare shape, steamed and re-blocked, twiddled and fussed and trimmed to one's liking, so that for less than half price, one had a new looking hat with fresh ribbons, flowers or feathers.

Once the generous Miss Ada had given the almost grown up Mary the gift of a beautiful new hat. Mary was staying with her august cousin in Crawford Square in Derry, and as a guest, she was unwilling to complain that the hat of Miss Ada's choosing was not quite of the shape she could wish. Its down turned brim hid her forehead and eyes, while it emphasised her lack of neck. Home again at Bridge House, Mary turned the beautiful hat round and round in her hands, wondering how best to make it more *her* hat. It was of a beautiful green velour with entwined ribbons of paler and darker green silk, infinitely too good not to wear, and yet, if worn, a whittler away of self confidence, quite the last role that a hat should play. In the end, she splashed out on the one reckless extravagance of her life. She took it to Gideon Baird's of Cornmarket in Belfast and there it became the thing of beauty it was always meant to be - so much so that Mary, by now light-headed, had herself photographed in it to preserve its beauty for ever.

Such extravagance was not commonplace for any woman round Ballyclare. The only extravagant female of whom the locals knew anything was the famous wife of one of the Langtry family who had lived for a time in Drumadarragh House. She was so beautiful and so extravagant that she was a creature of another world. Her postcard portrait was bought and admired by all. She was, it was whispered, on very good terms with his new Majesty, Edward the Seventh. She was the Jersey Lily, the most beautiful woman in this greatest age of beautiful women.

Mary's hat was not of the studied elegance of the Edwardian beauty's, but it was attractive and expensive and becoming - above all it did what a fine hat should. It made her feel good.

If a man were to buy a pair of boots in Ballyclare, he had a wide choice of quality and style. There were heavy boots for field work, there were fine pumps for Balls, there were clogs for foul weather, there were hand made brown beauties for Sundays and pressed cardboard mass productions for the poor.

Women had the same choice with the additional variety of buttoned boots, gutty (gutta-percha) slippers, and canvas shoes for summer that could be cleaned with whitening to give a fresh appearance. A good decent pair of everyday leather shoes for Mary cost six shillings - with an accompanying pair of white cotton stockings at sixpence. A good pair of hand made boots for men cost as much as twelve shillings and were well worth the money as they wore for years.

All leather boots and shoes were toed or heeled or soled at the cobbler's as they became worn, so that they went on for season after season, looking decent and keeping out the weather. There were two main kinds of protectors added to the leather soles and heels. Rows of sparrables were hammered round the edges to keep foot and footwear dry. Protectors, flat pieces of steel, were also put round in this way, with shaped demi-lunes of steel at heel and toe.

The sad shoes that troubled Mary's heart were those cardboard flimsies that imitated the style and dressiness of the upper classes but could be seen to disintegrate beneath the weather in a sudden deluge of rain.

A shoemaker made shoes. A cobbler mended them. Some tradesmen did both. The little boys in school had a song about the cobbler which they loved singing, because they could act it out at the same time.

> Oh, cobbler, I must have some shoes
> For mine are wearing out.
> My toes will soon be on the floor
> So make them strong and stout.
> The cob-bel-er raps,
> The cob-bel-er taps
> Upon his wooden last.
> With right good will
> He stitches still,
> His elbows working fast.

'As busy as a nailer' was one of the commonest terms to denote the industrious man. Sure enough, Charlie Cole the Nailer in Main Street was kept busy from morning till night, turning out nails of all shapes and sizes. The head of each nail was embellished with his initials, C C, and would last longer than his business. Jack the Nailer lived in a hut in front of Johnny Trimble's cottage at Kellystown. He was a little old man with shoulders permanently bent from leaning at his busy work. Mary never knew if he had another name. She took it for granted that he belonged in some measure to Johnny Trimble. Johnny was a rag man, gathering cotton and woollen rags throughout the countryside in his donkey cart which was laden with striped bowls, rosy mugs or plain white plates for barter.

In the town, watch makers too were busy men, but men busy with slow and skilled precision rather than with the fussy deftness of the nailers. Kennedy's, the jeweller's shop, was beautiful with a glittering array of real and paste jewellery, a cheerful, maddening ticking and chiming of clocks, a small, select display of hunters and half-hunters with Alberts in gold or silver for men, and delicate, beautiful pin watches for ladies, all hopelessly out of Mary's financial reach.

People with time to spare on their way to the trains would

46

stop at the window of Williamson the jeweller, who never seemed to sell anything at all. The motionless display in the dim windows, clocks, rings, brooches and bangles, grew only a little older, a little dustier, a little more Dickensian, as the years flowed by.

Saddlers, watch makers, dairymen, drapers, milliners, coach builders - every single solitary merchant depended, not just on the town industries of Bleach Green and Paper Mill, but also and to an even greater extent, on the hinterland of farms and rural industries.

Mary was delighted when it was possible in school holidays to contrive to be in the town on a Market Day. All the shops were usually busy, but the great business of the day was carried on in the open air. Besides the goods that changed hands in the Market House, the farmers had brought to town, driving them along the roads since early morning, sows, gilts and weaners, cows in milk and cows in calf, calves themselves and bullocks, occasionally a horse, a pony, a jennet or a donkey, and spring carts of cooped cockerels, pullets and old hens past the lay. The cacophony was deafening and unpleasant to town bred folk but music to Mary's ears. She did find the messy streets less to her liking but she was sufficiently a farmer's daughter to appreciate the value of the sweepings off the streets after the market.

If she could remain unobserved, there was no greater entertainment to her mind than the ritual dealing that went on throughout the day. Farmers in splashed brown boots and leather leggings, solid, if worn, tweed jackets and battered hats, strolled through the crowded Market Square, coming to rest beside animals in which they evinced not the slightest interest. This was a good time for a farmer to shove his ash plant under his oxter and pull out his pipe and his tobacco pouch. Cutting and rubbing the 'plug' ready for the briar, he would absentmindedly gaze at a cow that had just suddenly dawned upon his vision. Puff! Puff! Puff! went the newly lit pipe under the fire of the wax vesta. The man's eyes would slowly follow the smoke towards the sky. This was the point at which the owner of the cow would approach the potential buyer at a saunter, remarking on the state of the weather, the crops or some such noncommercial topic. Here stood two grown men, each of whom could read pretty accurately the mind of the other, communicating nothing pertinent to the bargain each hoped to make.

'The family all well?' says one.

'Bravely,' says the other. 'Can't complain.'

'Ay. Good. Good,' says the first.

'Late year the·year,' says the second.

'Lucky late,' says the first. Puff! Puff!

(Silence.)

'Not a bad baste there, ye brought,' says Number One. Puff!

'Though I doubt you'll have yer bother for nothin,' he adds.

'That's one of the best cows in the townland,' says Number Two. 'Bother for nothin' my fut! Onny buddy would jump at that cow.'

(Silence.)

'Ay! Ay!' says Number One. 'He wud luk a right eejit! Ha-Ha! Ha-Ha! Ha-Ha!' and slaps his knee. 'Jump at a cow! Ha-Ha!'

(Silence.)

'How· much are ye lukin'?'

(Silence.)

'Wudn't sell her this side o' thirty,' says Number Two.

'She's small in the elder,' says the first.

'Best milkin' cow I have,' says the second. 'Gran' milker.'

(Silence.)

'A wonder ye wud sell her,' says Number One.

'Over-stocked. Ay. Over-stocked the year,' says Two. 'And I wud like to bring the rest along like this'n, up to this class of a cow.'

(Master stroke.)

'Showin' her age a bit,' says One. 'What'd ye say tae twenty?'

Two laughs heartily. 'Man dear, ye like yer wee joke. Twenty - for a great wee cow like that? What'd ye take me fur?'

(Silence.)

'Twenty-seven ten,' Two adds absentmindedly.

One walks round the animal widdershins.

'She's oulder nor I thought,' says he. Puff! 'I might make it twenty-two?'

'Now, now, now, John,' says Two. 'I thought you were a man that knowed a cow when he seen one. There's a great wee cow. A bit o' the Jersey in her. Great milk. Great milk. D'ye know what I'm fur tellin' ye? If I wussint over-stocked and if I had tae keep one cow and one cow only, that's the very lady there.'

(Silence.)

'Twenty-six-ten, an' that's a gift.'

'Ay! Ay! Ay!' says John, 'might stretch tae twenty-three - but it wud be agin my better judgment.'

'Did ye hear what butter made the day, Robert Henry?'

'Six dee,' says Robbie. 'Harly worth the wife's time churning.'

'No, there's no money in the butter,' says John. 'Did I hear ye say twenty-four?'

48

'*That's one of the best cows in the townland!*'

'Ye did not. Just luk at that cow. Take a good long look at her. The more I luk at that cow, the more I'm in a mind to tak' her home again, but considerin' the wife's here wi' the spring cart and the bother it would be an' seein' its you that's a freen - I'll mak' it - ah - twenty-five ten an' that my last offer an' my han' on it,' leaving a great spit on his proffered hand.

'Right ye be, man,' says John, with a similar spit in his hand. They shake spitted hands sealing their bargain.

'An' I know ye'll not begrudge me the luck penny.'

With a 'luck penny' of ten shillings returned to the buyer after the sale, the cow changed hands at twenty-five pounds, the price that both buyer and seller had decided before the 'dale,' but this dealing and haggling was all part of the ritual of the market. It was fun for everyone and could be even more prolonged and entertaining if a third party thrust himself into the act as intermediary just for the hell of it, as Alfred would have said.

That market day in nineteen hundred and four was particularly memorable to Mary because it was then that she saw for the first time the men employed to clean the streets, sewers, and privies of the town and care for its other few amenities, open the door of the Master's old two room Residence - the ground floor of the former National School - and emerge with shovels and brooms. Downstairs stayed the implements. Upstairs in the former school room sat the new Councillors in their Council Chamber. For the very first time Ballyclare had an Urban Council and the new Council had begun its first work. And thus for almost seventy years public spirited men and women would so serve their town. And why wouldn't they? Did they not start off under the very best adviser Ballyclare could offer, their first Town Clerk and the children's old friend, Mr Ned Hill?

Although Mary was occasionally in the town on Market Day, she was never once permitted by Aunt Laetitia to go to the May Fair.

So she went.

She didn't go until she was all of sixteen years, and should have obeyed her Aunt and should have known better. But she was then a strange, stubborn and obstinate girl, and almost the surest way of making her do something was to tell her not to. She could see no reason for not attending the May Fair. She did ask Aunt Laetitia why, but all she got was compressed lips and the prim assurance that no lady would be seen dead at the May Fair. Mary hadn't any intention of being seen dead anywhere, and she sadly suspected already that she was no lady, therefore Aunt Laetitia's reasons carried no weight. Nevertheless, thought Mary, subterfuge might be better than a row.

Under bottomless buckets up-ended over some crowns, Aunt Laetitia grew delicate early pink rhubarb in her half acre plot of this healthy vegetable. This forced offering was a very special gift for very special friends. Mrs Ferguson got some, the Rector got some. Now Mary made her plunge. 'Do you still want somebody to take Mrs Herron's rhubarb over to Grahamstown?' she innocently asked her truly innocent aunt. All schools were on holiday for the Fair.

'That boy!' said Aunt Laetitia, becoming suddenly cross. 'I do believe there's nothing but nonsense in his head. And very strange friends he has too, some of them,' she added darkly. 'But he should have remembered Mrs Herron himself. She really *is his* friend.'

As she raised her tiny figure to its full height and flung away, Mary translated this correctly as a scolding for the absent Lennox who was 'that boy.' After digging in his heels (which no one could do better) about discontinuing his formal education, Lennox had gone with his job problem to the Rector. It would have been the last recourse Mary would have considered, for the Rector was, if possible, even less knowledgeable about the world than Aunt Laetitia. However, Mary was quite bowled over to find that Lennox was suited right away. Earlier, as she and her brother had strolled by their river on a spring evening, Lennox had told Mary all about it. Mr Major had given him a letter of introduction with a strong recommendation to a Mr Magee who had a nursery garden near Ballyhackamore.

Lennox had gone off to Belfast cheerfully to start learning to be a landscape gardener, as he thought. He had visions of himself as the twentieth century's Capability Brown. True to form for any apprentice, he started at the bottom, pricking out endless seedlings, carrying hundreds of watering cans each day, hoeing and cultivating up and down rows until it seemed his back would break. He had his fill and more than his fill of it all. Lennox had learned from Hughie Hull that work was as rhythmic as any other activity of nature. When Hughie dug, he moved easily from the down thrust boot to the side flung soil and back to the soil. His rhythm of rise and fall was enclosed within a further pattern of labour and rest, labour and rest. Lennox knew that Hughie laboured efficiently because he rested efficiently. Every few minutes Hughie would lean on his spade, breathe evenly, relax every muscle and gaze intently at the land about him, absorbing it in love. Len found now that if he followed Hughie's advice of labour and rest in his endeavours to be a good cultivator, his master's voice, harsh and embittered, rasped at him across the nursery rows. 'And what do you think you're at, my fine young gentleman? Leaning there looking up to Heaven - a place you'll never see!'

Mr Magee was a man of that deep Ulster piety which allowed salvation to none by the Elect - and Len had definitely not been elected. Instead he had gone cheerfully on his way to the everlasting bonfire as that accursed creature, a Bohemian.

In Bloomfield, where he boarded in Belfast, he had speedily made friends with three young brothers who lived nearby. They were Herbie, Billy and Charlie Corr, gifted commercial artists at David Allen's. They introduced Len to their work mate and bosom friend, Willie Connor, while Len in his turn introduced them all to his friend, Stanley Wilson. Stanley was a cadet member of that Wilson family who owned the Doagh Flax Spinning Mill, and was no linen merchant except under compulsion. He was, instead, an enthusiastic amateur mechanic of the internal combustion engine, and all his spare time was given to his novel and adored possession, a motor cycle. This had a side car of basket work in which Mary made her first ever journey by motor power, complete with motoring cap and veil.

It was soon the custom for all six young men to get somehow into or on to Stanley's motor bike and take off for the week end to Bridge House, where politeness induced Aunt Laetitia to make them welcome even as she eyed them askance. Mary, who should have had sense by now, went off into her old giggles at the picture of Stanley, still shaking violently from the prolonged vibration of his machine, graciously taking the tremulous finger tips Aunt Laetitia extended to him, and they both shook together in a way that was unintentional. No sooner were the lads all indoors and fed, than they and Mary and Little Sister and Frederick retired to the drawing room and the old piano there. Almost everyone could both play and sing. Only Mary had to sit idly by and admire with shining eyes, with Willie Connor (about to drop an 'n' and become Conor, the first step on his way to being the eventual doyen of Irish painters), who was worse off than Mary even, being tone deaf. He, too, was desperately ambitious to be musical, and with the help of his friends and the family, did learn by rote one tune on the keyboard - 'The West's Awake.' That splendid black head, that fine profile, those dark brilliant eyes of Conor, all glowed and shone with an ambition realised, as his strong sensitive right hand struck out a mal-fingered melody line of passionate sentiment while his equally strong sensitive left hand, not knowing what the right was doing, maintained a steady thump, thump, thump on the C below middle C. His happiness was complete. His ambition realised. He never learnt another tune, but sat back happily sketching his friends round the piano, where, immortalised by him, they remained for ever on paper, to be hung for evermore over Mary's mantelpiece.

When they didn't come to Bridge House - and, indeed, Len could not impose his 'very strange friends' on Aunt Laetitia too often - all the young men set off on their unreliable transport to their seventh heaven, a little labourer's cottage at Craigavad. They all clubbed together with yet two more artists, Gerry Burns and Gerry Arneill from Allen's, to pay the infinitesimal rent and to buy food. Here they did as they pleased, from Saturday lunch until very early Monday breakfast. They slept, basked in the sun, drank beer, painted, drew, talked, sang, talked, played and talked. Occasionally, Mary was privileged to be present. It was Bridge House all over again, for their first priority in furnishing had been a sixth hand piano. But it was gay and light hearted and filled with sunshine even in winter, for there was no Aunt Laetitia in Craigavad!

When Lennox from time to time came home alone instead of cavorting off to Craigavad with the other Bohemians, his first port of call was invariably Herrons' farm at Grahamstown. He loved Mrs Herron like a mother. Her mother had known Pappy and this made a bond between her and his children. They were all welcomed in this warm happy home, and none more so than Lennox. Who can now say that it was not, perhaps, a little on account of that pretty daughter of the house, Jean Herron?

Jean's father, Frank, was a farmer who worked with desperate intensity to wrest the best living he could from his land. He was a quiet man, a little lugubrious, given to no frivolities. His wife was jolly, a warm hearted woman with a ready laugh and a cheerful welcome for all comers. Perhaps her husband thought she needed a little keeping down. Perhaps she thought he needed a little lifting up. So throughout the happy simple family life ran a quiet feud at which Mrs Herron took what she called her 'dead end.'

Her farm house was comfortable, warm, welcoming. But - it had no parlour. She determined to have a parlour. Frank determined she wouldn't. She won. Week after week, she earned a little pin money from dress making, baking, jam making, quilting - everything at which she could turn her hand. And the great day dawned when she (not literally) broke her way through the kitchen wall to the adjoining byre. That doorway opened the way for a byre to become one of the prettiest parlours ever seen. By great good fortune Mary chanced to call when it was just completed. She had never seen such happy pride and satisfaction on anyone's face as she saw on Mrs Herron's whilst together they gazed on the fresh plastered walls, new made window and scrubbed deal floor. It was as yet unfurnished, but it was a wonderful, wonderful parlour.

As was to be expected, Frank Herron voiced no opinion on his wife's accomplishment, though Mary was sure that his face showed a faint glimmer of pride in his newly acquired parlour. His wife laughed heartily at his lack of enthusiasm. She knew him very well. And, like every wise wife, allowed him eventually to come to the point of thinking it was all his own idea. She kept her own counsel. He worked hard, and sure if he wanted a parlour, wasn't it nice he had got one?

Mrs Herron's favourite joke about their kindly feud concerned her delft dogs. It was fashionable, almost compulsory, to have a charming pair of delft dogs to guard either end of a kitchen mantelpiece. Mrs Herron had no dogs. She decided to have dogs. Back she went to her stitching and baking, her chicken rearing and egg collecting. Gradually the sum in her china teapot grew to the necessary four shillings, then the wages of two children for a week's long work in a mill. When the donkey man came on his monthly visit, she proudly bought her dogs, washed and wiped them till they gleamed, and set them in their appointed places.

Home came Frank from his work in the fields. He loosed the hames on the plough horse and entered his newly embellished kitchen. His lack-lustre eyes fell on the dogs, while the family stood round, awaiting with bated breath his verdict. Slowly he turned each dog round and round, and eventually upsidedown. There on the bottom of each was a large figure Two. 'Wise woman again!' says Frank. 'Fourpence more lost!'

It was to Herron's farm, therefore, that Mary so kindly offered to take a gift of rhubarb. Aunt Laetitia, oblivious of the Fair's enchantments, nay, of its very happening, tied up a welcome parcel of the pretty pink sticks, reflecting that Mary was improving. Definitely becoming more considerate.

Over the fields by the Granny's Knowes and the Thorndyke,

Mary skipped like a galley slave suddenly freed. She spent no time with her dear old acquaintance, Grannie Mellon. To be truthful, she spent little with her dear old friend, Mrs Herron. She dumped her rhubarb excuse on the latter's kitchen table, enquired rapidly for everyone's health, saw how the Begonia Rex was progressing and was off. As she neared the town, the blare of the steam organ already beat the air. Talking, shouting, singing, walking, shooting, trotting, bell ringing, ware calling - the noise of the Fair was made up of almost indistinguishable parts.

Dazed and dizzy, Mary made her way through the crowds in the Market Square. The hobby horses rose and fell to the rat-a-plan of mechanical drummers on the calliope. Ballymena Jean shouted her wares - 'Har' nuts 'n' yella-man! Har' nuts 'n' yella man!' Hard nuts were excessively hard biscuits of the consistency and apparent age of the pebbles in Mary's river. Yellow man was a sticky, hard honeycomb toffee that had to be chipped off with a little hammer.

'Dullies! Dullies! Fresh Dullies!'

Dulse was edible sea weed, salt and tangy at first, but soon turning to a rubbery mass of tastelessness that had to be got rid of discreetly when no one was looking. One of the country sayings Mary made little sense of was - 'Ye're doatin' for dullies and the dullyman's deid.' Did anyone ever make sense of it?

Mary took in all around her till her head throbbed. Gipsy caravans, horse dealers, tinkers, knackers, find the lady men, shooting ranges, stalls for delft, flowers, cabbage plants, boots and shoes - the great gathering-together of the annual May Fair was bewildering. Mary was determined to make her sin worthwhile, so she gaped and absorbed until it seemed she breathed in the very steam of the hobbies, the perfume of the flowers, the ammonia of the droppings, the sweet treacly odour of the sweetmeats, and the rancid wild smell of gipsies and tinkers. It was wonderful. She would always know now what the May Fair was like. She was glad she had come.

'What in the world are you doing here?' said a gentleman's voice in an ungentlemanly scream above the cacophony. Mary turned. It was Mr Ferguson. She flushed with guilt, but William John's brown eyes twinkled.

'May I give you a lift home, ma'am?' said he with a little mock bow.

Mary nodded her head violently and then regretted it, for it throbbed with noise, tension and guilt. She followed her guardian to the livery stable. He led out his spanking horse and trap, held open the door for her as though she had been a real lady and not a silly disobedient girl. They made their way slowly against the crowd in the Main Street, even more slowly through the Market Square and emerged into the comparative peace and quiet of the Doagh Road. From her vantage point in the high trap, Mary had another good look at the Fair. She didn't see it again until she took her own children there to see the same scenes. But what she remembered most about her adventure was the gentlemanly kindness that got her home in good time and asked no awkward questions. What a *nice* man Mr Ferguson was!

Chapter 5

The summer of nineteen hundred and four brought the ever-blessed school holidays. One whole year of her five successfully accomplished, Mary felt happy for the first time in months.

She and Little Sister both had their birthdays in July but now one birthday party had to do for both. If it was slanted so much to the younger girl that it actually took place on her natal day, Mary didn't mind at all. She had several very good reasons for this - not the least of which was her affection for the short sighted Little Sister whose future was so precarious. She also felt an adultness about helping Aunt Laetitia prepare a party for 'the children;' added to all this was her emergence from Pappy's year of mourning.

Mary had been provided with a single garment to make this great stride forward. Aunt Laetitia had presented her with a pretty summer blouse of white voile, sprigged with pale blue forget-me-nots. Its gigot sleeves ended in eight inch cuffs with tiny pearl buttons. With her black skirt well sponged and pressed and her boots brilliantly polished, she felt a little stir within her of what she might have called Miss-Waide-ness. That blouse was really quite becoming.

After her year of steadfast mourning for her dear brother William, Aunt Laetitia seemed suddenly to break from a black chrysalis into what was, for her, the existence of a social butterfly. First of all came that party. No one had had any social life since they were in black, so even the boys took an interest in the birthday, Little Sister's twelfth. She was to be allowed to invite whom she would. Lennox, Frederick, baby Moxie, Aunt Laetitia, Little Sister - that meant six already. Aunt Laetitia suggested three more children. Little Sister agreed and went into contemplation of her rather limited circle. She decided almost at once. Her dearest friends first of course, the three little Ferguson girls nearest her own age, Kathleen, Molly and Leeby. 'Good!' said Aunt Laetitia and began counting dishes and cutlery in her head.

'Wait a minute,' said Little Sister suddenly. 'I can't leave out the Kelly boys - Montgomery and Tommy and Charlie. They are nearly my best friends.' So with only a momentary hesitation, Aunt Laetitia took this in her stride. For Little Sister she would do almost anything.

'Right,' said Aunt Laetitia. 'Yes. I expect we could manage that. Now that's two and two's four and two's six and three's nine and another three's twelve. Well! Well! I expect we'll *have* to manage it,' and she unbent in one of her infrequent smiles.

'And we'll have shortbread like Mrs Ferguson makes and jelly and cake and some apple tarts and snow-tops and ...' Little Sister was planning too. •

'We won't have anything of the kind,' said Aunt Laetitia. 'A cake, yes, a wholesome plain cake. And it will be bread and butter first and no cake till that's eaten.'

'Oh!' said Little Sister, the party suddenly losing some of its richness. Aunt Laetitia looked at the soft little face that was slightly crestfallen. She felt a whim of indulgence.

'Well, now,' she ventured, 'if you could have just *one* thing for your party what would it be? Now I'll let you have *one* thing.'

Little Sister's face suddenly lit up from within and the winsome eyes sparkled.

'I know what I'll have. Now you promised, didn't you?'

'Certainly I did,' said Aunt Laetitia, rather stiffly.

'Then I'll have the McKinstry's for they are my next best friends. Joanna and Bob and Sam,' and Little Sister laughed gleefully at her own triumph.

The battle did not stop at these few exchanges, but Little Sister could wheedle and coax and cajole, and soon Aunt Laetitia could be heard going about the house saying '... and two's six and three's nine and *another* three's twelve and *another* three's fifteen. And bread and butter first and that's final!'

Mary liked the idea of fifteen round the dining room table for it meant enlarging it to its fullest extent, just as it used to be when she was only six and mother was alive and jolly and laughing and always having lots of cousins and aunts and friends and acquaintances staying or calling or feasting. Now no mother, no Pappy, no Alfred. Mary dashed a cowardly tear away that had sneaked up on her suddenly, and applied herself to the task in hand. It was ever the best way of forgetting trouble.

The day of the party dawned fresh and bright. Mary was to wonder afterwards why Little Sister's birthday parties always took place on sunny summer days. It wasn't possible. Yet in retrospect, that was how it was. Little Sister, as the birthday girl, was up at dawn wandering about in the glad early sun and feeling excited. Something prompted her and she went round from the yard to the front of the house where the scarlet ramblers and purple clematis scrambled up the walls and bay windows by the front door. She tried to pick some to garland her table but found the task beyond her, for the sappy stems refused to break. Back she went round to the kitchen again and returned with Aunt Laetitia's scissors.

Mary was always an early riser, and she was just coming downstairs as Little Sister came in by the back door, her birthday posy in her hand. Mary's heart contracted at the sight of the flowers, for they brought back in one dreadful rush the Will reading after Pappy's death that had left them poor in pocket and so much poorer for the loss of Alfred. A glance at her sister's happy face enabled her to reach out a gentle hand for the flowers. She put them in water in a cool stone jar by the sink. Together the sisters breakfasted on tea and toast and marmalade.

Clumping little feet coming down one step at a time told them Moxie was on her way.

'Come on,' Mary called and poured out a cup of milk. The baby toddled in at the door still in her long nightdress, bare feet on the flagged floor. Mary lifted her on to her knee and the three had a womanly breakfast together and a chat. Wild whoops and throat clearings came from the bed room above where Aunt Laetitia was in purdah. Lennox was home on holiday. He and Frederick still slept the sleep of the just - or the unjust, depending on one's viewpoint. The three young ladies let them sleep. They had other fish to fry.

Lunch was a scrappy meal that day for the youthful guests were expected at three o'clock. By two, all dishes were cleared and washed, the house swept and garnished, and the big table prepared as far as possible. Aunt Laetitia had qualms about putting out mother's wedding china, but reflected that Kate would have put the dishes out herself for the children if she had been alive, and so salved her conscience against any possible breakages. The feast consisted of plates of white and brown bread and butter, three kinds of jam no less, and the *cake*. Fresh raspberries from the garden with such cream as Lennox had not filched from the crocks would round off the meal. The cake had started out in life as a very plain slab from the O.P.B. but Lennox was nothing if not artistic. He put a large side dish in the middle of the table, put the uninteresting slab on the dish and surrounded it with the beautiful flowers. Now he was beating hard at some cream skimmed from the milk crock. Whipped cream tinted with a little cochineal was his intention, but the beating was a divil of a job as there was no separator.

'Oh well,' he reflected, licking his fingers, 'if we don't have whipped cream, we'll have pink butter,' and he went on beating.

His perseverance had its reward and so had the cake, for the centrepiece of pink cream cake made all the visiting youngsters go 'Ooh!' and 'Aah!' as soon as their eyes fell on it. It had, in fact, only one drawback as a cake. Little Sister couldn't eat it. She had a monumental allergy to cream and butter. But all that was as nothing in her eyes compared with the glory of a pink cake garlanded with flowers! They could eat it all and welcome. She had the glory.

At the huge table with mother's best china and silver teapot sat Kathleen, Molly and Leeby Ferguson, and Montgomery, Tommy and Charlie Kelly, and Joanna and Sam and Bob McKinstry, to say nothing of Aunt Laetitia, Lennox, Frederick, Moxie and Mary. Little Sister reigned as queen for a day, a position which she was not slow either to enjoy or remember.

Aunt Laetitia was not really at her best at a children's party table. In honour of the occasion she had donned her best black silk gown, hooked and buttoned all the way to its low tiny waist. Above its high neck sat a frill of white tulle while, to keep her head even more erect, around her neck she wore a black velvet band fastened with a cameo brooch. Her scanty hair was not merely scraped back today into a bun on top of her head but actually had a puff by either cheek bone and a fringe on her forehead, rather frizzy from her curling tongs. A jewelled tortoise shell comb held her back hair in place. Mary, gazing at her Aunt as though she saw her for the first time, noted the strength and determination in that small lined face, and, more-over, saw the pretty young girl her Aunt must have been, at say, the outbreak of the American Civil War or even the Crimean War. Suddenly she felt ashamed that her Aunt immediately brought battles into her head. It could not have been easy for Aunt Laetitia, and here she was smiling and making halting, if conde-scending, conversation with children whose ages ranged from nine to thirteen (for Mary didn't include herself with 'the children'). Thinking of her Aunt's real sacrifice, Mary determined to be Good, a resolution she made weekly, sometimes even daily.

'Can I pass you some blackcurrant jelly, Aunt?' she said gently.

Aunt Laetitia bent an immediate glance of suspicion on Mary for she could never read what went on in her niece's head.

'No, thank you. I already have some,' she said shortly, and indicated the healthy spoonful of jelly at the side of her plate.

Mary promptly stopped trying to be Good and felt a fool instead, which her Aunt had always suspected anyhow. Why was it that she couldn't even do a little thing like that right? She almost gave way to one of her depressed fits that so often alternated with her feeling of elation-for-no-reason-at-all, except that all the world was suddenly hers for the taking. Pulling herself together, she tried again.

'Can I help you to something, Molly?' she asked.

'Cake, please,' said Molly Ferguson, who liked her food. 'My mother said just to take one piece, so could you make it a good big one?'

Mary grinned at Lennie, who promptly cut Molly a double-sized piece. The pretty little girl with hair like golden corn sank her teeth into the pink cream with satisfaction, swallowing with it a purple petal of clematis.

'Me too, please,' said her *alter ego*, Leeby, just eleven months Molly's junior and her closest friend and admirer. 'But not so big, I'm full up. Nearly.'

Kathleen, the oldest Ferguson girl, was admiring her convex reflection covertly in the silver teapot. She, too, was twelve, like Little Sister, and already showed promise of being a very beautiful woman. Her hair was a rich, bright chestnut, and her skin lush peaches and cream. She was lovely. And already she knew it.

Joanna McKinstry, between Little Sister and Mary in age, was in charge of her two young brothers. Dressed rather stiffly for the occasion, they sat like Tweedledum and Tweedledee eating steadily all that Frederick urged upon them on one side, as he did on the three Kelly boys on the other. He had a strong fellow feeling for hungry boys. And when was a boy not hungry? Joanna shot several warning glances at her two charges, but as they paid no attention and were eating silently, she gave up and went back into the ladies' conversation.

Aunt Laetitia had already enquired from each family the condition of its parents, grandparents, sisters, brothers, aunts and uncles and had come to a full stop. Her attention now was taken up with eyeing the food apprehensively, wondering whether it would or would not go round. It was certainly going very fast. She glanced at Lennox, who was devoting himself to

61

slicing away happily at cake, or passing bread and jam and making entertaining remarks enjoyed by the whole table. He caught his aunt's enquiring, worried look, interpreted it correctly and signalled back with his eyes towards the hall. What did the boy mean? Aunt Laetitia raised her eyebrows. This time Lennie sketched something in the air and even went so far as to jerk a thumb towards the door. Aunt Laetitia's eyebrows descended abruptly into a frown. Lennox passed plates like mad, saw everyone stoked up and the table almost clear of food. He laid a friendly hand on Mary's shoulder as he passed, and went into the hall. He put nothing but his arm back round the door holding aloft a brown paper parcel.

Aunt Laetitia grunted with relief. She had forgotten that there were good things brought by the guests, sent by very understanding mothers. Mary had followed the charade with some amusement. The sentiment helped her to make another effort at Goodness.

'It's all right, Aunt,' she said. 'I'll go with Lennie,' and excusing herself, she left the sunny table and galloped along the passageway to the back regions.

Already Lennox had opened several gifts. Mary recognised at once Mrs Ferguson's marvellous shortbread. She and Lennox immediately ate two pieces each. It was altogether too good to waste on children. While they ate companionably in the long, cool pantry, they sliced a rich currant loaf from Mrs McKinstry and piled on plates fresh scones, still warm, from Aunt Minnie Kelly. Bearing their trophies in triumph, they re-entered the dining room. Appetites that had begun to flag took on a new lease of life.

'Let's get the rest ready and we can enjoy ourselves too,' said Mary to Lennox.

'Right you are, ma'am,' said Len. 'Fred, see all the boys are looked after.'

Frederick, with a mouth full of jammed scone, nodded like a mandarin.

'And you too, young lady,' said Lennox to Little Sister. 'Look after your visitors.'

'So I am,' said Little Sister indignantly, stung by such an unnecessary hint when she was doing so well.

'All right, all right. You're the best hostess in the whole world,' and Len escaped with Mary back to the pantry

'I wonder if I left enough damn cream,' he said, gazing at the milk crocks. At eighteen now, he sometimes used words like that out of earshot of his aunt.

'Plenty, plenty, plenty,' said Mary blithely, throwing down pudding plates all along the bottom shelf. 'I say, doesn't this for all the world look like Smithfield?' (Not the London Meat, but the Belfast Variety Market.) There were four white plates with navy blue and gold bands, there were five white porcelain plates, each with a scattering of raised purple violets, another five willow pattern plates and several variegated soup plates that would do for family.

'You do the fruit. I'll do the cream. I'm good at this now, I've had some practice today,' said Lennie. Mary took the bake bowl of raspberries that she and Little Sister had gathered before lunch. She started going along the row of plates.

'Two for you, and two for you, and two for you ...' As she passed each plate, she dropped two raspberries in. Wisely, she backed from the window to the door, reversing down the row again. 'Three for you, and three for you, and three for you ...' Up and down she went, providing fair shares for all until the bake bowl had nothing but a few raspberry hairs and a little pink juice at the bottom.

'Waste not, want not,' said Lennox succinctly, supping the juice with a teaspoon. Now he would get to work. Every dish of raspberries he topped with cream from the crocks, and there was quite enough to give the dishes of fresh·fruit the festive touch they needed.

'I'll start,' said Mary, and, putting six dishes on a big japanned kitchen tray, walked carefully with it to the dining room. Frederick heard her two gentle kicks on the door. Why wouldn't he? Wasn't he listening for them? Mary passed the raspberries and cream to Little Sister who happily passed them in turn to the ladies. Baby Moxie cried for some which she couldn't have, and was silenced with a fat stick of shortbread.

Back came Mary with more raspberries and cream on the old tray, Lennie bringing up the rear with the family plates. He delved in the sideboard drawer and brought out mother's silver dredging spoon. The little crystal bowl of caster sugar sat ready to his hand on the sideboard.

'Sugar, sir?' he said in his best waiterly manner to Tommy Kelly. Tommy couldn't answer among the various embarrassments of giggling at the joke, shyness at being asked, and masticating at the same time his lovely currant loaf. Lennox wisely took silence for consent, dumped bowl and spoon in front of Tommy, urging him to get on with passing it round.

Little Sister surveyed her table. It was a wonderful party. Things really should be like this far oftener. Now who had a

63

birthday next and they'd have another party? Yes, of course, Aunt Laetitia. Only they'd have to wait six whole weeks for it.

'Auntie,' she said (and she was the only one of all the five children who ever addressed her aunt in this way), 'let's have a birthday party for your birthday. It would be lovely. Third of September. It would still be nice then. Oh, let's have another party just for you.'

'When you're my age,' said Aunt Laetitia tartly, 'you'll stop having birthdays at all. Now get on with your raspberries.'

After the birthday feast the sun was already moving from the hot, hot south to the beautiful west. The children were freed from the formal table and allowed to leave the house by the informal back door. Once into the yard, they cast from them the shackles of good manners and quiet behaviour that parents had imposed on them before they left home. Aunt Laetitia retired to the drawing room alone, pulled down the holland blinds to keep out the sun, and permitted herself the ladylike relaxation of reclining on the sofa. She was doing what she called 'thinking with my eyes shut.' Mary and Lennox and Frederick carried all the left over food and the dirty dishes from the dining room and prepared for a large washing up when all the guests should have gone home. Lennie brought the dining table down to its usual size, replaced its usual red chenille cover, drew the blinds against the sun and retired to the back yard with the damask cloth and its crumbs. He shook the crumbs to the frenzied hens who dashed hither and yon, realising that something good was somehow passing them by. He returned with the shaken cloth to Mary who had put away all food and to Frederick who had stacked all dishes. Ruefully, they looked at Mother's best table-cloth. Her dishes and glass and silver were intact, but the lovely cloth with its double woven design of roses and shamrocks was blotched and stained like a child with the measles. Splashes of raspberry juice, droplets of jelly, dots of jam, faint mani-festations of 'pink butter' showed in colourful drifts on the white surface.

'No help for it,' said Mary. 'Into the washtub before those stains set.' And she scraped off the buttery marks. Into cold spring water went the tablecloth, and as it turned out as good as new when laundered next day, one might say that the feast was safely over without a single catastrophe.

Fred, having stacked his dishes, was not too grown up at fourteen to play with the children. He rushed out by the back door the minute his stacking was finished. In a more leisurely manner as befitted their maturity at sixteen and eighteen, Mary and Lennox too joined the young fry in the farm yard.

Already the grass showed green on the hard surface where grass had never been allowed to grow in Pappy's day. No horse in its stable, no crop in its field. At least not the children's crops. They belonged to whoever took the land which was to let each year. One solitary cow, Daisy, still lived with the Bridge children, having her feast of meadow grasses undisturbed by any other bovine or equine creature. Alone she waded from the wet meadow's edge into the river. Alone she drank. And when she came into the yard at milking time, swinging her full udder and lowing gently, she had no company in all the yard but the twelve hard-working hens and one loud-crowing cock.

This was what was left of Pappy's dreams.

Len kindly went along with Freddie to show the other boys the pigeons. They toiled up the ladder into the barn loft, now inhabited only by the birds, the few mice and rats that escaped Pussy's or Carlo's clutches, and the motes that danced in a sunbeam. The pigeons were those, and the descendants of those, given to the boys several years before by Uncle Joseph. Uncle Joseph lived at Castlerock on what might be called the Home Farm. It certainly was still Home to Aunt Laetitia.

The pigeons as usual did not disappoint, but flew in and out of their open aviary in the roof space of the barn, or strutted importantly about the wooden floor. There were handsome pies, fat-breasted pouters and elegant dove-like fantails. They always put on a show for guests.

Lennox watched indulgently when he should have been reprimanding Fred for showing the Kellys and McKinstrys the other attraction the barn offered. It had a second door, opposite to the one by which they had entered. It unlatched from inside and there, just an arm's length away, was a looped rope over a huge pulley. This had been used for hoisting sacks of grain from ground to barn level. The Bridge children had long ago discovered that the door of this upper room was a marvellous jumping off place. It was twelve or fourteen feet from door sill to ground level. When Pappy had forbidden this pastime to his madcap family, they obeyed as they obeyed all his commands. They found the pulley-hoist a more-than-adequate compensation. Now Frederick in the true spirit of hospitality was giving Monty Kelly first go at descending to ground level by the hoist. Monty, in his sailor suit, was not sure if he was doing the right thing. One look at the suit and another at the hoist were enough to make up his mind for him. He stepped nimbly into the loop, hung on for dear life, and Fred lowered away. A laughing face from below showed how Montgomery enjoyed his treat. He raced round to the ladder to mount into the barn for another go. In the meantime, away went Tommy, next went Charlie, then Bob, then Sam. Down the hoist and up the ladder went the continuous chain of boys, shouting and puffing in the hot, dusty air, working hard at their play.

As a refinement, and a breather for himself, Fred showed them another method of descending, whereby they could hold the lowering rope and let themselves down. This was taken up with enthusiasm by all the male guests. Lennox, now bored with the game and dying to play it himself, betook himself to social safety with the girls being shepherded up the Big Field by Mary and Little Sister. All the visiting girls were taking turns at carrying Baby Moxie who didn't want to be carried at all. She struggled in vain for they were all determined to be little mothers. Lennox, coming up, rescued her and set her astride his shoulders, she holding on tightly round his forehead with her tiny hands while he held her by each little ankle. Off he went galloping up the Big Field while Moxie squealed with delight and the other girls begged for a pick-a-back. Just one, just one. Please! Please! But Len knew when enough was enough. He put young Moxie down on the ground again, took her baby hand and invited Mary to show her prowess as a teacher by organising something for the others. On her mettle, she soon had them playing tig, from that to hide-and-go-seek round the warm, dry ricks of hay, and so finally to that delicious game, so unpopular with all farmers, climbing up and sliding down the ricks. Lennox put a stop to this and they all drifted down towards the house again to collect the boys for a visit to the river. What a sight met their eyes!

Sure enough, the lads were having a truly happy afternoon. They were scarlet and sweating, their hands were blistered, their clothes were almost unrecognisable from the dust of the barn floor and the rope, to say nothing of the odd toss taken on the dirty lane.

'Jumping Jehoshaphat!' said Lennox. 'I say, you fellows better come with me for a minute.' And he bundled them into the back hall, with severe strictures about noise.

'Take the others over to the burn,' he said to Mary, 'and I'll clean these gents up. Be with you in two shakes of a lamb's tail.'

By the river, the westering sun cast long shadows of the bridge and the trees. It was startlingly pretty as the ashes and willows drooped their many leaves by the spears of the sagans. All the young ladies sat down on the bank in their party frocks and divested themselves of white stockings and buttoned boots. The hot little feet found pleasure in the cool grasses, and Moxie tried to catch butterflies with her toes. Little Sister was the first to cast off from dry land and wade into the ice-cold brown water.

'Oh!' she screamed, for the cold was unexpected. Molly and Leeby promptly joined her and they screamed in unison. Joanna joined in the fun, and they all started searching for horse-leeches so that they could scream again. Kathleen sat down on the grass by Mary and together they made a daisy chain for Moxie who would put only a timid toe of each foot in the water. The other Daisy ambled over to greet them, swishing the eternal flies with her tail. Lennox, coming across the meadow with some tidy, brushed and washed boys, took in the picture - the summer river, the pretty girls chattering like charming magpies, the pinks and blues and whites of party clothes, his sisters that he loved, even old Daisy - a silly, little unimportant scene, but it was home to him for ever.

No sooner was the birthday party over than Aunt Laetitia announced that she had a further treat for the two girls. It was a secret. But if they paid attention to her and did their work and minded their manners and generally got into no scrapes, she would tell them in good time. What on earth could it be? The two girls puzzled and wondered.

'We're getting a new cat, or maybe a new dog?' thought Little Sister aloud.

'Nonsense,' said Mary. 'Carlo wouldn't allow another dog here, and we have five cats as it is and more coming If I know anything.'

'Oh, is that so?' cried Little Sister. 'More pussies? Still, if you know, then Auntie must know too. So it can't be that. Maybe it's a new dress?'

'No money,' said Mary tersely.

'S'pose you're right,' said Little Sister. 'Maybe Aunt Fletcher's coming to see us after all and maybe she'll bring us something nice?'

Aunt Fletcher was Aunt Laetitia's Good and Rich sister who had Good and Rich children. She had lately ignored this little brood of relatives who did her no credit.

'Not a hope,' said Mary. 'And who wants *her* anyway?'

'Well, I do,' said Little Sister, 'for cousin Maud has perfectly beautiful dresses and satin boots and fur muffs and all sorts of things and she's very big now and she must have loads of ... of ...

of ...' Under Mary's eye she faltered.

'Hand-me-downs! From her?' said Mary. 'A fine treat that would be!'

And the mystery remained a mystery for nearly three weeks, with Aunt Laetitia receiving a constant barrage of innocent queries, helpful hints, tricky questions and one or two sorrowful tears, to all of which she displayed a blind indifference.

At last, with August, came Aunt Laetitia's news. She had a little money saved from her small private income, and as a treat for herself as well as for Mary and Little Sister, she had decided to take them to Portrush.

'Portrush!' said Mary, as if it were the end of the earth.

'Portrush!' said Little Sister, beaming, as though it were Ultima Thule. And the two sisters took hands and did an impromptu dance round and round on the kitchen flags.

'Stop that nonsense at once,' said Aunt Laetitia, 'or you won't go at all.' But there was a kindly gleam in her eye, just the same. 'We're going because I have saved for it, and because they are running an excursion train from the Upper Station. Half-a-crown to Portrush and back. So pray for fair weather.'

'And get your clothes ready,' she added.

Aunt Laetitia really had broken out that summer, for here was their very first excursion. This was to become an annual event. Having provided for the care of the others at home, Aunt Laetitia was taking Mary and Little Sister only on this Arabian Night's voyage.

Mary's voile blouse came out again. Again the boots were polished till they glittered. Again was the black gored skirt sponged and pressed with great despatch. With this outfit and a straw boater, Mary was ready for the end of the world. Aunt Laetitia got Little Sister into what had been Mary's cream linen suit worn in honour of Sir George White's triumphant return to Ballymena after Ladysmith. The emerald-ribboned straw hat was still perfect, if too childish for Mary. Aunt Laetitia got herself ready in her good green serge that was still her good green serge since days of former ease. A basket was packed with a fine assortment of sandwiches and bottles of home made lemonade. At last, they were ready for the road.

The road it was, too, for the first part of the journey was a walk to Doagh to mount upon one of John Steele's side cars. For sixpence return fare, Jock would whirl them to their broad gauge train at the Upper Station, and be there again at night to bring them back to the village, for, although it was called Doagh

Upper Station, it was two miles out of Doagh.

For Mary, the holiday began as soon as they climbed on the car. The old horse trotted willingly in the gentle morning air. Although dull, hazy clouds filled the sky, it was a warm morning, with a promise of sunshine to come. Dobbin slowed to a walk when he passed the Palantine National School, for he had a steady pull before him to the red brick station itself. Mary could see another of Steele's cars in front of them further up the hill, and yet another coming behind. As well as the three other travellers on their side car! It was obvious that they weren't going to be the only folks setting out for Portrush that day.

At the Upper Station, they dismounted and bade John and Dobbin a temporary farewell and set their faces towards the little booking office. With careful shillings and pence, Mary purchased the three excursion tickets, for Aunt Laetitia did not care to perform such responsible tasks which were really the prerogative of a gentleman. Being no lady, Mary found little difficulty in being a gentleman, at least temporarily, and counted out the three half-crowns as grandiloquently as though she were the Earl of Doagh. Really, there were times when Aunt. Laetitia - shush! Mary put the thought away and deliberately made herself think of that elderly lady's sacrifices instead.

With a screeching of brakes and slow chuffs from the engine, the excursion train drew up at the platform. Aunt Laetitia suddenly displayed remarkable agility and was first into an empty carriage and seated by the window facing the engine. Mary took the seat opposite, promising to change places frequently with Little Sister, who seemed quite satisfied just to sit there. In spite of Aunt Laetitia's efforts, their carriage was invaded. The three excursionees who joined them were old Mrs Mooney and her sons Johnny and Tom from Drumadarragh. Aunt Laetitia was prepared to recognise Mrs Mooney, who also regarded herself as a cut above the ordinary. The ladies exchanged slight bows and the boys and girls rude stares. The boys were indeed young men, even if they were being taken out for the day by their mother.

For Aunt Laetitia, the time passed pleasantly in desultory conversation, and all the ladies were glad of the gentleman's help in changing trains at Ballymena and again at Coleraine. Mary was always certain that at Coleraine she could smell the sea. It was just a fancy from her childhood, when going to Coleraine meant going on to her father's family at Castlerock for a holiday. The train to Portrush puffed at last into its seaside station. They had arrived.

Taking the fore-way of Mrs Mooney, Aunt Laetitia bade her and her sons a gracious farewell and left them. It was possible that they were going to eat in a hotel, and Mary's family would eat sandwiches by the seashore. One had to make little economies to achieve even an excursion treat, but there was no point in pushing these things down everyone's throat.

To stretch their legs and get rid of their travel weariness, the elderly aunt and her two gauche nieces walked smartly from the station along Portrush's Main Street. Without a halt, they walked till they were at the furthest possible extremity of Ramore Head. There the everlasting breezes of the Atlantic blew away the last school cobweb from the brains of Mary and her Little Sister. Aunt Laetitia stood for a long time on the Head, gazing along the coast in the direction of Castlerock on the other side of the River Bann. All of this north coast was her territory, and she loved it with the intensity of attachment to a piece of mother earth that is possible only to the Irishman and the Israelite.

Having adored her Lares and Penates, Aunt Laetitia turned with softer face than usual to the girls.

'Come,' she said. 'Let's look at the shops in Main Street.'

A happy hour's dawdling down one side of Portrush Main Street and up the other brought to view not only some lovely clothes, jewellery, silver, cakes and boots, but the more exotic and specifically watering place offerings - souvenirs. Mary and Little Sister exclaimed over the pleasures and prettinesses of them all. Although they did not hope to buy, they got a deal of pleasure from just looking. 'Window shopping,' Aunt Laetitia called it. There were seaweed frames, shell boxes, a multiplicity of fine chinaware for what-nots, often emblazoned with the Arms of the town and the legend 'A Present from Portrush,' so that one could prove one had been there. It was fatiguing work, this window shopping, and Little Sister was not slow to announce this, especially with a prompt from Mary. Aunt Laetitia was in a softened mood, induced by breathing the air she loved. She agreed immediately and they all betook themselves to the Strand, walking just far enough to be by themselves.

The smooth stones and the humpy stones, lying here and there in the huge stretch of sand, were warm to the touch. With a little searching, they found suitable seats among them. Aunt Laetitia produced her fine laundered handkerchief and ordered the others to do the same. They spread out their upholstery thus and seated themselves. From under the half-lid of her basket,

Aunt Laetitia produced a clean tea towel, three thick tumblers and a bottle of lemonade. Opening the other half-lid, she handed Mary a packet of sandwiches in a damp cloth and a similar packet to Little Sister. Mary's were lettuce and cress from the garden, Little Sister's hardboiled egg. All this food they could produce themselves and it was no novelty, but somehow partook of a novel quality in these surroundings. They handed and swapped the sandwiches back and forth, swilling them down with lemonade. All three were hungry now that food was in sight. Mary, the 'far lands filled,' leaned back happily on her warm rock and gazed dreamily at the Skerries. Here it was, she thought, that the emigrant ships of a hundred and fifty years before had lain at anchor. In the shelter of these rocks had rested the Ulster Scots setting out to create the true America. Larne had been the only emigrant port in Ireland then. She wished very much to see two things now she had at last arrived in Portrush, or to see one and hear the other. The latter was the bell of the Methodist Church. The Earl of Antrim had forestalled Mr Ned Hill nearly a hundred years before by giving a site to the new Wesleyans. That famous Wesleyan, Dr Adam Clarke, whose memorial obelisk stood in the town, had a gift of the bell from the Duke of Newcastle who had earlier had a gift of it from the Czar Alexander, Little Father of All the Russians. Mary felt her historical happiness would be complete if only she could hear the bell. She never did.

Her other heart's desire was to see the place called Port-na-Spaniagh round the coast towards the Causeway headland. Here, so legend said, was lost the great Spanish Armada galley, the 'Girona,' which had held not just the flower of the treasures of Spain but, more importantly, the young flower of her nobility. Being storm-steaded on those Antrim rocks, there had perished two hundred and sixty young noblemen of Castile and Aragon and their brave commander De Lyra, all washed ashore and buried near their great ship, lost for ever. But not everything was lost, it seemed, for there were things Mary could never hope to see - the cannon that the sons of Somhairle Buidhe salvaged for their Dunluce Castle, and two great chests of iron in the Castle of Glenarm, all that was saved from the 'Girona.'

Luncheon and rest time over, Little Sister indicated to her aunt that she would like to 'go a place.' The girls often assured one another that Aunt Laetitia must be a hen since she never, never, wanted to 'go a place.' There was no public convenience to hand, so all three ladies wandered swiftly in the direction of the White Rocks where they would find the privacy they required among the many caves and boulders. Mary wanted to see Long Gilbert and the Brock's cave and the Piper's cave and the very, very romantic Smugglers' caves, but as Aunt Laetitia didn't know which was which, she had to be content with her general idealised impression of that coast. Rested, relieved and refreshed, they walked briskly back by the Atlantic breakers to the town to take the Causeway tram, the earliest known electric train, that would take them to see, for the first time, that wonder of the world, the Giant's Causeway.

Some people were already aboard the tram which was preparing to set out on its voyage of pleasure. Aunt Laetitia hitched up her little bustle with her left hand and stepped out nimbly as only she could when pressed. The girls extended their stride whilst avoiding an outright run, and all were on the train in time. Their carriage had neat little toast rack seats, open sides and a roof. In the other carriage, they suddenly caught sight of Mrs Ferguson and family, also evidently out on excursion. With a deal of fussing and swapping of seats and obligements from other passengers, the two families got together.

'Here goes,' thought Mary. 'Now they'll talk all the time, just when I'm wanting to think.' And she steadfastly turned her face to the sea and floated out of the conversation.

To Mary, that little train was the world's wonder. It had everything, the convenient, the healthy, the picturesque. Mary was quite certain - and never had reason to change her mind - that no transportation in all the world had such a romantic and beautiful route. All the gibble-gibble-gabble coming from the others couldn't distract her from absorbing with passionate delight all she saw.

Suddenly, disaster thrust itself into their innocently beautiful day. From the side lane of a farm, a man was approaching the main road along which the little train trundled merrily. He was on the inland, the train on the seaward side of the road, so that the train was in no way responsible for the horror that happened so swiftly. The man was leading a farm horse, a huge Clydesdale. Where his lane debouched on the roadway, there were rocky banks on either side. Foolishly, he led the horse from the offside, so that as he turned right into the road he was between the great horse and the rock. For some reason he slipped. In seconds it was over. The body lay there, still, by the rocks. Now the gleaming bloody iron hoofs of the Clydesdale were still too, where moments before they had thrashed and pounded in sudden fear. The loose horse shivered, its shiny body twitching with

'*To Mary, that little train was the world's wonder.*'

73

terror.

Mrs Ferguson screamed, and then subsided into a low reiterated caoine. Mary felt white. Little Sister was motionless, wide eyed. Aunt Laetitia's hand had tightened its grasp on a seat rail, but she uttered not a sound. Two men, evidently locals, sprang from the Causeway tram and waved the driver on. Gladly he removed his load of holidaymakers from the scene of disaster. The moments of shocked silence passed and suddenly everyone was talking at once. How terrible! How dreadful! The relief of words was already helping folk back to normality, but no one there on that day would ever forget the so-quick tragedy. Even Mary, who had very much wanted to think herself into the tragic history of the McQuillins of Dunluce - mainly on account of her old friend Mrs McQuillin of Cogry - and into that romantic tale of Amergin, bard to King Conor MacNessa at Bushmills, forgot her nonsense. Her mind was a blank. She didn't come to herself until they were actually on foot, descending to the Little Causeway. The great 'Honeycomb' of the Middle and 'The Loom' of the Great Causeway caused her little more on this trip than a dull wonder.

'Look,' said Aunt Laetitia, who 'owned' the Causeway. 'See the Giant's Punch Bowl.'

'Look. No, over there. Look, you stupid girl. Over there. The Giant's Organ. The Theatre. The Chimney Pots. The Wishing Chair ...'

Only this last really gave the girls a thrill that day, when they had to come out of their stupor to think what they could wish for. Mary thought and thought while the others urged her to get on with her wishing so that they could have a turn. Pressurised, Mary played for safety in immediate matters.

'I wish,' she confided to the hexagons and pentagons, 'I would pass all my exams. Especially the Needlework.'

Chapter 6

Mary glided into the second year of her Monitress-ship as the seasons flowed imperceptibly by. She had now become accustomed to her role and to the hard work which it entailed. Some things she had found very difficult, but these were the by-products of the educational system rather than any aspects of her study. It was hard at first to stand all day long. She could never understand why a teacher could not, say, tell a story while seated just as well as while standing bolt upright. Tell it even better, perhaps? Such a thought was heresy, to be put hastily from her. In her very first week, the Master had taken care to point out to her in the Inspector's Report Book a damning indictment of a former needlework teacher. The words under the Master's pointing finger remained with Mary for ever. 'The children brought their needlework up to the teacher. SHE SAT.' The capitals had been heavily under-scored.

It was wearying, too, to work hard in school all day and then go home to household chores and a full night's study. In time, as she grew a little taller, a little stronger, this difficulty grew less and less, until at last she felt she could even take an occasional break.

She never got a break from the greatest plague of all - the time table. This could never be changed. The Medes and Persians were easy-going compared with the Irish Board of Education. Even if pupils were good in one subject and weak in another, one could never rob Peter to pay Paul. Each subject did not have only its allotted hours per week but minutes per lesson, and that autocratic beast, the time table, brought any activity to a full stop on the dot, even though children and teacher were together happily engrossed in their subject.

A few seconds before the end of each half hour period, the Master stood with deliberate bell in hand. Lifting the tongue, he struck a few decisive chinks. Miss Waide rushed to the harmonium, and to the strains of 'The Battle Hymn of the Republic,' the whole school rose as one and marched left, right, left, right, to the next position of sitting or standing in its proper place in its proper room. This mad dash to the instrument took place every thirty minutes. It must have imposed a considerable strain on Miss Waide as she flew to wheeze out a jolly march within split seconds of hearing the despotic chinks.

Not only the classes, but all slates, books, pens and pencils moved by numbers. In the long desks, as the Master prepared his warning tocsin, books were passed from right to left towards the passageway for collection. The pens went on their rhythmic journey too. Objects were accompanied by a chant from the high priest for their ritual movement - one, pens *down*; two, books *close*; three books *pass*; four, arms *fold*! It was fortunate that no pupil ever did anything that could by any stretch of the imagination be called creative, for the one, two, three, four would have intruded as mercilessly into the composition of an ode as into the boring Penmanship or Transcription.

With Mary as Monitress, the Master's little staff of three was completed by the musical Miss Waide and the stern Miss Allen. Both were excellent teachers, tolerably popular with all pupils and enthusiastically admired by a few. Lennox's first love was Miss Waide. For her, he saved his pennies and bought a miniature book, much in vogue at that time as a bracelet charm. Most of the pupils did not have quite this much devotion to either lady, and called them Punch (Miss Allen) and Judy (Miss Waide). This was no reflection on the teachers' relationship with one another, which was of the most amiable.

Miss Waide was a soft person. Her hair was light brown and fluffy. Her skin was like that of a peach, faintly tinted and downy. Her clothes were exquisite, for she had plenty of money and a deal of very feminine taste. She tended to the ruched, frilled and lacy school of thought. When her glance occasionally encountered that of the Master, she dropped her eyes and flushed delicately as a moss rose. Mary admired her very much.

Miss Allen was, on the other hand, a little darker, a little older, a little stricter, a little less obviously charming. She wore a long, dark skirt, shiny buttoned boots, a white shirt blouse with leg o' mutton sleeves and a striped silk tie. She, too, had her admirers, especially among the senior girls who tried to emulate her standards of needlework, particularly in spoking, drawn thread work and all forms of flowering or embroidery.

Both ladies taught the three R's methodically and conscientiously. Their more junior pupils would eventually pass into the Master's care and he would be aware of any slacking. His word and his opinion were absolute. No despot ever held more sway over his kingdom than the school principal of that era. He, in turn, feared only the dreaded Inspector, the enemy of one and all. An Inspector's job was to find something wrong. He nosed around the closets (if any) just as readily as he pried into the work of teacher and pupils alike. It was an easy task to perform. An Inspector was not there to help. He was there to find fault. He invariably found it.

When the time of Inspection fell upon the School, a few children were tactfully encouraged to absent themselves, even though the teachers' salaries depended upon the number of pupils present every day. Not only did they have to be present but they had to know something. The earlier payment-by-results system was iniquitous. Each teacher's pay then depended on the results of the Inspector's findings as he delved into the three important aspects of learning, seeking any possible opportunity for failure.

As a young child in Doagh National School, Mary met one such Inspector and remembered him ever after with a peculiarly strong dislike. He had given out his test in Arithmetic. Mary was quick and accurate. She knew she was right in her test. She folded her slate to the bosom of her frilled white pinafore, her sums done, all correct. Her classmates on either side were struggling gamely, finding the going hard. Mary glanced at them pityingly, feeling more than a little pleased with herself. Suddenly the Inspector pounced. He wrenched Mary's completed slate from her enfolding arms. His saliva flew venomously as he made a furious nought on every correct sum. 'That,' said he, 'that will teach you, young madam, not to copy.'

Copy, indeed! Mary was angry. Not only had she not copied from her neighbours at whom she had glanced, but she had had no need to copy. At the time she was bitter, tearful and rebellious. In later years, she came to resent the incident even more when she learned that, because of those unjust noughts, her teacher, her dear 'Flinging Jenny,' would receive no money for teaching Mary Arithmetic.

For each pupil passing in this subject, Miss Laird received two shillings and eightpence. The same sum was paid for each pupil passing in Reading and again in Writing, so that for passing in the three R's, a child was worth eight shillings of her teacher's annual salary.

Mary had almost cost Miss Laird another two-and-eightpence

on a different occasion. This was at the Advanced stage when older pupils above the statutory leaving age of eleven had to do an instant composition for the Inspector under his eagle eye. 'Flinging Jenny' with shaking hands doled out the official sheets of paper to every pupil. She prayed that they would all write *something*, although an immediate flow of English prose was never easy for Ulster children.

'One side of the paper only,' said the Inspector. All fell to with a will, for pupils were often good natured and generally obedient. Some chewed their pencils, wrinkled their brows, laboriously wrote with tongues protruding in concentration. Mary had never found any difficulty in expressing her thoughts. Her mind was lively and perceptive, her penmanship fast but regular. On she went progressively to the foot of the page in neat paragraphs set in one inch from the edge with neat margin running down the left hand side. Turning over the page, she went racing on, her busy pencil flying across line after line of the second side of the precious sheet. As she glanced ceiling-ward for momentary inspiration, she caught sight of poor Jenny's face, strained and white, staring at her in desperation. With sudden fainting heart, Mary realised her sin. She had written on both sides of the paper. The dreaded Inspector advanced, looming over Mary. Miss Laird faltered an apology, an attempted explanation. Mary raised her downcast eyes courageously to the bearded face. Suddenly the Ogre smiled. 'Let her fill both sides if she can,' said he. 'And,' he added, 'give her another page if she wants it.'

Perhaps he seldom got lengthy compositions. Whatever the reason for his kind and unusual breach of the Sacred Rule, he redeemed in Mary's eyes the whole Inspectorate that had fallen to despicable depths after the fiasco of the sums. He must, indeed, have noted that the child had some genuine interest in language, for later he called her up to stand beside his knee at Miss Laird's Table and expound to him the story of brave little Vera who walked through the snows of a Russian Winter, pursued by wolves, to carry a Reprieve to her father in far-off Siberia - no mean feat. This was a favourite story in the Third Book. By the time she had reached the Sixth Book, Mary was confident enough in English to query aloud the opinion of David Garrick concerning her beloved Goldsmith.

'Here lies Nolly Goldsmith, for shortness called Noll,
Who wrote like an angel, but talked like Poor Poll!

Her success in English composition and reading had obviously gone to her head, only to be smartly slapped down now in these present Monitress years when, for her King's Scholarship, she found she was going to have to commit to memory not only most of *Macbeth*, *The Merchant of Venice* and all of Milton's *L'Allegro*, but also Nolly's complete *Deserted Village* and *The Traveller*! This formed a small part only of the English course. This subject was taken very seriously indeed by the Irish Board. Teachers were expected to know things. They were not expected to think, but they were certainly required to *know*. Everything was to be learned by heart - Joyce's Irish History, British Constitutional History, the Physical and Political Geography of the World (no less), Music, Drawing, Penmanship, Arithmetic and Mensuration, English, Reading, Poetry, Drama, Composition and Literature, Household Management and the ever-ghastly Needlework at which Mary was no better now than she had been as a child. One failed the whole King's Scholarship Examination, a pre-requisite to training in Dublin at Kildare Place, if one failed in any one of the 'Failing Subjects' - English, Arithmetic, Music, Drawing, Needlework or the all-important Penmanship. Mary feared nothing but the Needlework. Now from Miss Waide and Miss Allen she was striving to learn to make sense of the old bloody 'specimens' she had done for 'Flinging Jenny,' that kindest of creatures, and woolliest of teachers.

So with the Senior girls, doing needlework in the Big Gallery next to the scutch mill, Mary learned to do all that would be required of her in the Practical Examination in Needlework at the end of her apprenticeship. Miss Allen was kind and patient, and demonstrated over and over again the types of specimens required. Miss Waide taught Mary various sorts of fancy-work, but as this was not needed for the examination, she paid it scant attention. She was neither nimble nor artistic. She did, however, learn to make an unbelievably ugly lamp mat in wool. This had a flat crocheted circle of vari-coloured wools worked with a medium hook, surrounded by a fat, gathered fringing made with a large crochet hook. As an *objet d'art*, it had nothing to commend it, but Mary did become proud of it seventy years later when she learned that Charlotte Bronte had made just such a mat for *her* lamp! Even this tenuous literary connection would have reconciled her to needlework for ever if only she had known it at the time.

Three Rachels sat near Mary in the Big Gallery - Rachel Wright, Rachel Hoy and Rachel Agnew, with Agnes Phillips, their friend. These were the most senior girls who had stayed on

79

at school after the official school leaving age, soon to be raised to twelve years. They were, like Mary, furthering their education, but their great and real interest was in fancy needlework. They were charming girls with long plaits of shining hair and soft voices full of Irish chatter. They would stay at school until they were perhaps as old as fifteen, when they would leave, put up their hair, lengthen their skirts and wait to get married. Sitting in the Big Gallery with these happy, gently gossiping girls, and under the kind supervision of Miss Allen, Mary made her very first garment. All articles of clothing made in school were called, not blouses or drawers or chemises, but 'garments.' This kindly euphemism spared the blushes of the modest children, though in truth Mary never knew one of these. She was more likely to hear instead the occasional hair raising language of children escaping from school, the happy children racing to fields and trees and freedom. But she had learnt from her life with Aunt Laetitia that the still tongue makes not only the wise child but the even wiser teacher. The blind eye and the deaf ear were added to the still tongue. And this was the first teaching discovery Mary made for herself. It was not the Master's way, but it was ever her way, and so it remained for fifty years.

This first garment was to be a blouse. Mary felt excited, for it would be lovely to own another blouse. She had little confidence in her ability to produce anything wearable. She fixed her faith instead on Miss Allen and in due time faith had its reward. Her teacher purchased two yards of the prettiest and finest woollen material Mary had ever seen, of a clear scarlet merino with a pattern of little white circles. Together they measured and cut and tacked. Under that kindly eye, Mary did her very best running and hemming. The soft material was gathered into a flat yoke. The long sleeves ended with six inches of tightly buttoned cuff. The neck, wonder of wonders, was not high and stiff but of an advanced fashion of soft roundness. To trim all and give a professional finish, Miss Allen's purse produced a yard of finest white ruching to edge the soft neckline and the fashionable sleeves. If one did not examine the stitches too closely, that blouse looked really well. Mary wore it with pride, and never missed an opportunity to mention casually that she had made it herself. The pennies she saved to repay Miss Allen for the material were as nothing. The gratitude she felt towards her teacher was the real payment. It is likely that Miss Allen, a perceptive and kindly woman, knew this.

As Mary sat during what was now, for her, the happiest time of the week, the Needlework Class, she could hear the busy hum of the school. In her gallery, gentle soft gossip and the click of steel knitting needles fashioning black socks and stockings were all that could be heard. It was most restful, yet full of brisk and happy industry.

From the Big Room in the middle of the school, she could hear the Master's middle Classes 'doing history.' Standing with their toes to a chalked semi-circle on the dusty wooden floor, they were performing their chant-by-rote of the sovereigns of England, while senior boys sat, every head industriously bent in the long desks, doing extra arithmetic and mensuration while the senior girls sewed. They were oblivious of the chant.

'Willyumthe conkrer	-	Tensixtysixteneightyseven
Willyum roofus	-	Teneightysevenelevenunderd
Henrythfirst	-	Elevenunderdeleventhirfive
Matilnstephen	-	Elevenfiffoureleveneightynine
Henrythsecon	-	Eleveneightynineelevennninetnine
Richarthfirst	-	Elevenninetninetwelvesixteen
John	-	Twelvesixteentwelveseventytwo
Henryththurd	-	Twelveseventitwothirteensevn
Edwardthfurst	-	Thirteensevnthirteentwensix
Edwardthsecon	-	Thirteentwensixthirteensevenysevn'
Edwardthethurd	-	

and on
and on
and on.

Mary knew all her dates too. She supposed they were history, but she was rather glad that at home the Bridge House's many bookshelves held Dickens' *Child's History of England, A Tale of Two Cities, Ivanhoe, Children of the New Forest, Kenilworth* and dozens more books with interesting historical backgrounds, to say nothing of her beloved *Child's Guide to Knowledge* that still afforded her amusement, or Thomas Tegg's *Historian's Companion* that gave her even more fun. Who could not enjoy a companion who told you that Archbishop Ussher had computed the Creation as having taken place at nine o'clock in the morning on Sunday 23rd October in the year four thousand and four BC? Tegg contained so many gems that he truly was fit to be anyone's constant companion.

The middle classes rhymed on. Bees buzzed in the sunny windows of the Big Gallery. Robbie Blakely, the young cobbler who lived and worked on the high ground that sheltered the back of the school so closely that it was level with the top windows, left his hut. He left his cobbling shop that was half a wee sweetie-shop and strolled in the June heat to peep in at the Big Gallery window to see the young misses sewing. Miss Allen shooed the mischievous lad away, and he strolled back to his whitewashed thatched cottage to lean at the doorpost, gazing from his height out over the brilliant lush countryside, over the river and the high-banked dams to the Cogry Mills that had founded the school years before, and over the mills to the blue Cave Hill far beyond, shimmering in the summer heat.

The day was so fine that Miss Waide had taken her classes out on the cassie for Drill. The infants had gone home at two o'clock. The rest of the school was busy with the Master or Miss Allen. Miss Waide's First and Second Classes of boys and girls were obviously much happier outside than confined to the four ledges of the Low Gallery. They carried their little dumbells with them. Mary could just see the neat rows of seven and eight year olds swinging their shiny dumbells in the afternoon sun. 'Up, down, out, down, up, out and down.' The pleasant sound of Miss Waide's voice could be heard through the open window. The dumbell drill was followed by Physical Jerks, well named. The little arms jerked up in the air and down and out and in with the grace of marionettes. Miss Waide was a most unlikely Sergeant Major of her little Army, with her soft manner and gentle eyes. She even perspired daintily.

The sound of the children moving from the rough ashy ground back to the Low Gallery meant that Miss Waide had observed from her gold pin-watch the time drawing near for her harmonium performance to close the half hour. In the Big Gallery, the seniors returned their needlework to cotton work bags, and stored them under the lidded back seat of the gallery. The middle classes ceased their chant. The Senior Boys passed one, two, three, four, their arithmetic and mensuration books for collection. The whole school was drawing together for the final period of that and every day when they would all join in the Big Room under the Master's baton for singing.

It would be difficult for anyone in later years to realise the musical standard reached by these pupils of a poor rural and even poorer industrial background. Barefoot lads and freckled farm girls, half-timers and little social climbers all found themselves caught up in one of the Master's passions, Music. They read Tonic Solfa at sight when they found difficulty in reading English of the same standard. They sang rounds and canons. They sang in two, three and four parts. They followed immediately the swift pointer moving up and down the modulator or

'They sang in two, three and four parts.'

along a sight test. They interpreted unhesitatingly the Master's hand signs for pitch or for time. They poured forth in glorious singing the 'Theme sublime of endless praise' of Handel, the 'Morning Prayer' of Mendelssohn, Mozart's 'Ave Verum,' Telemann's 'Holy, holy, holy' and, feeling no descent to the ridiculous, the rip-roaring or bathetic works of Moody and Sankey, so dear to the Master's personal religious life. 'Where is my wandering boy tonight?', Mary reckoned, was always good for a tear or two at a Service of Song, while 'Bringing in the Sheaves' could equally lead to ruder rhythmic floor stamping by the undesirables in the back seats. School singing did not only provide an exciting finish to every school day, but also a life-time's interest for all who passed through the Master's hands. Might one not dare to say that for this gift to his children, much that was narrow, canting, rigid and severe in him would be forgiven?

Chapter 7

'December of nineteen hundred and five brought its climax, in its usual way, to the school year. The official year might begin and end in summer, but the children's year followed that of the calendar. December was the end of the year. December was Christmas. December was the School Swarry. Mary was ever to remember that particular year, for it was the first time she met the peculiar manifestation of hostility that can emanate from the Parent. The School Swarry was, like Gaul, neatly divided into three parts. First, the children ate, drank and made quietly merry, for no raucous behaviour was possible until their later release into the cold night air. Next came the Concert, provided by the pupils. Finally, the highlight of the evening arrived with the Prize Giving of medals and books, provided by the mill owner.

Adam McMeekin owned the Cogry Mills. He was a stocky, energetic little man with shrewd eyes, coarse features and a dark, scrubby moustache. He stood a good five feet tall in his shoes, and could arouse terror in the hearts of men and women a head taller than himself. Behind his back he was the 'Wee Buddy,' this last being merely Ulster for 'man' and certainly *not* American for 'friend'. He was kind in his way. He saw that his school was always supplied, from the mill, with coal for heating and soft soap for cleansing. From small beginnings he had become a mill owner, a land owner and a cigar smoking businessman, with a pleasant mill house in Ulster and a town house in London.

It seemed but a short time since he had arrived at the Cogry Mills for managerial training under the then owner, his brother William. He had been a small, slight youth, child of an Ulster farmer as Mary herself was. Sheer drive, ruthlessness, ambition and charm had placed him on that pinnacle of prosperity where Edwardian mill owners, as *nouveaux arrivés*, were forgiven much because they had the money to buy much. William had acquired an accomplished English governess to bring up his children in the highest tone. Adam married her, and Miss Clements brought up not just his children but himself into reaches of English society he could scarcely have dreamt of as a youth. His children did not go to the school he heated with his coal and cleansed with his soft soap. They had, instead, not an English governess it is true, but a French Mademoiselle and a German Fräulein. The Master was commanded to the schoolroom of the mill house to coach the mill owner's children in the three R's. Polish was acquired abroad. While girls left the Mill School to finish their lives at the spinning frame, Adam's two daughters were finished with lessons in music and dancing. While Mary struggled with, even as she delighted in, her Goldsmith and Corneille, 'the Wee Buddy's' son went to acquire his veneer at Heidelberg, in those far-off days before Wilhelm of the withered hand had shown his other hand too clearly.

For the School Swarry, all was bustle in the Mission Hall. Row after row of clean school children faced the little platform with its varnished front rails and steps. On the platform the Concert and Prize Giving would take place. In the meantime the tables and chairs were useful to hold the tin trays lined with thick, unbuttered slices of juicy currant loaf and mugs painted with roosters and roses, filled with sweet, thick brown tea. Only the children would eat. Parents did not share in this part of the proceedings. The mill family would not share in it either, but would arrive in time to occupy the front seats at the Concert, having dined in some splendour at home.

This year their gleaming barouche had been left in the coach house, and a strangely named new building was a 'garage' for a horseless carriage. They would shortly arrive in this glittering monster driven by the former coachman, John Gibson, now a liveried chauffeur.

Miss Waide perspired in her usual ladylike way as she fluttered about in pink chiffon frills and lace trimmed corsage of velvet roses. She was responsible for the Concert, and the Paris Opera could have held no more excitement and tension in its artists than Miss Waide had to manage in hers.

Mary knew her job to a nicety. She was the dogsbody. The tea was prepared in Mary Smith's house in the little Brookfield Row opposite to the Mission Hall. Mary was to supervise the senior girls carrying their brass kettles of tea from Smith's to the Hall.

Outside in the dark, sparkling night, hopeful parents had

arrived early. Beggs Robinson, one of the mill foremen, was the Keeper of the Door. Even though parents should not really come in until tea was over, early arrivals could count on a kind hearted Beggsie to let them in from a bad winter's night. A rope stretched across the aisle separated the rows of children in front from the parents behind. Early parents sneaked silently into seats to which they were not entitled for another half hour. They gazed at the walls in admiration. From end to end they were covered with examples of beautiful needlework pinned up by the girls. Sheets of paper in various colours had been tacked to the boards, and against the blue and pink and scarlet, the drawn thread work and crochet of the white linen cloths showed their perfection. From the finest handkerchief with its hem stitching and edging of crocheted lace to the largest cloth flowered in most intricate embroidery, they were magnificent examples of needlecraft that would be heirlooms to the third and fourth generation.

More parents gathered outside the now firmly closed door. The 'Wee Buddy' would arrive soon. Beggsie leaned against it confidently. They should not pass.

The favoured parents within waved as their children's faces turned to them, grinning mouths showing half-chewed currant loaf, moist with delicious tea. The press without became menacing, and Beggsie's door was threatened with assault and battery as snow flurries appeared from nowhere. Mary wondered about her charges and their tea kettles. The Master nodded towards the back door in the dressing-room. She took the hint, slid out by this door, ran across the road to Mary Smith's. Good! The last supplies of tea were almost ready. She warned the girls about the snow while urging them to hurry. As she crossed again to the hall she was aware of people. They were huddled in a dark, shapeless crowd at the main door, shawled heads covered from the winter's cold. Suddenly, one of the women spied her in the light from Smith's door.

'Look at *her*! Who does she think *she* is?' shouted the woman suddenly. She was fractious with frustration and with waiting in the cold darkness after a long day's work in the mill. She wanted to see her children. She longed for the exciting colour and entertainment. Here was a young brat of a girl, small and skinny, sailing in and out of doors as though she owned them. The others took up the cry.

'Look at *It*, going out and in.'

'It's *our* weans that's in there.'

'*She* gets in and we're shut out,' and much more in a worse vein until obscenity reared its ugly head.

The shouting and the sudden violent menace frightened Mary. She was very shaken. She almost believed that they would strike her, for she could not at the time understand the coldness of feet that had stood bare in even colder water all day at a spinning frame, nor the immense desire of all the women for the other-world of a concert, for an evening's pleasure. Trembling, she pushed herself in again at the dressing room door. She had met the violence of a frustrated crowd and it had frightened her. That was all. Beggsie had seen all and said nothing.

Soon the tea was over. Every last mug was handed up, sticky with sugar. Some children ran to their parents in the back seats. Mothers spat on handkerchief corners and cleaned up rosy faces and rough little hands. The shining children raced back to their seats as the doorman let in the horde of potential Mesdames Defarge - but now they were quiet, tired, rather timid women, overawed by the glamour of a lighted hall and the exotic promises of excitement to come. Their voices were low and occasionally they giggled nervously or stared around with a false boldness.

The shining motor car of the McMeekin family drew up at the door of the Hall. The small group of lads and men coming to the Concert had deliberately waited outside to see the monster close at hand, to have esoteric conversations with John Gibson, and to acquire expertise that would be displayed with pride and off-handedness at work. Horseless carriages were the most magical of news.

The Family was greeted by the Master and a respectful silence. The former Miss Clements sailed regally to the front row. She, like her husband, was small of stature, but robust and rosy. She wore a black winter suit of fine barathea, the skirt touching her polished toes, with a three quarter length coat having an exaggeratedly sprung waist and deep hem of astrakhan. On top of this stout, genteel little edifice was a very smart, very wide black silk hat with plumes of osprey. Her husband followed in black velvet-collared coat, high white collar and bow, his Homburg in his hand, wafting incense of Havana. Then came the two daughters, favoured by fortune, in pretty dresses. The Master brought up the rear. As they all edged themselves into comfortable positions, Beggsie tiptoed respectfully to whisper to the 'Wee Buddy.' The latter whipped round sharply and gazed for a moment at the offending women. He and Beggsie then looked across to Mary. The 'Wee Buddy' smiled reassuringly. Mary smiled back, unsure of what she was supposed to do or

'The shining motor-car of the McMeekin family drew up at the door of the Hall.'

to have done. Miss Waide seated herself at the harmonium and the Concert began.

The Concert showed within its little confines the influences of many lands. Chiefest of these was the great British Empire itself, then at the scarlet zenith of its glory and power. But close behind came the influence of Ireland and Scotland (each in its own right), and of Japan and America. Amid the barbell and dumbell drill came the recitations and action songs that brought those breaths of other lands.

The young McMeekins first performed graciously the pieces taught them by their governesses and, having shown how things should be done, settled back in their seats, as enervated and relaxed as common children after the ordeal.

One of the most favoured of all recitations to find a place in the programme was a spoken duet between a soldier and his mother. Privately, Mary thought it a stupid poem, not only for its stumping doggerel, but because the mother did not recognise her own offspring. However, the audience loved it. It was an old tale.

Mother: O come you from the Indies, and soldier, can you tell
Aught of the gallant Ninetieth and who are safe and
well?
O soldier, say my son is safe - for nothing else I care,
And you shall have a mother's thanks - shall have a
widow's prayer.

Soldier: O, I've come from the Indies - I've just come from the
war,
And well I know the Ninetieth, and gallant lads they
are.
From Colonel down to rank and file, I know my
Comrades well,
And news I've brought you, Mother, your Robert
bade me tell.

Mother: And do you know my Robert now? O, tell me, tell
me true!
O, soldier tell me word for word all that he said to
you,
His very words - my own boy's words - O tell me
every one!
You little know how dear to his old mother is my son!

90

Soldier: Through Havelock's fights and marches the Ninetieth were there;
In all the gallant Ninetieth did, your Robert did his share;
Twice he went into Lucknow - untouch'd by steel or ball,
And you may bless your God, old dame, that brought him safe through all.

Mother: O, thanks unto the living God that heard his mother's prayer,
The widow's cry that rose on high, her only son to spare!
O, bless'd be God that turn'd from him the sword and shot away,
And what to his old mother did my darling bid you say?

Soldier: Mother, he saved his Colonel's life, and bravely it was done;
In the despatch they told it all and named and praised your son;
A medal and a pension's his; Good Luck to him I say,
And he has not a comrade but will wish him well today.

Mother: Now, soldier, blessings on your tongue; O husband, that you knew
How well our boy pays me this day for all that I've gone through!
All I have done and borne for him the long years since you're dead!
But, soldier, tell me how he looked, and all my Robert said.

Soldier: He's bronzed and tanned and bearded and you'd hardly know him, dame,

(Huh! thought Mary in the wings)

We've made your boy into a man but still his heart's the same;
For often, dame, he talks of you, and always to one tune
But there, his ship is nearly home and he'll be with you soon.

91

Mother:	O, is he really coming home and shall I really see My boy again, my own boy home? And when, when will it be? Did you say 'soon'?
Soldier:	Well he *is* home; keep cool, old dame he's here!
Mother:	O Robert! My own blessed boy!
	(Crash, the dawn breaks! thought Mary sourly)
Soldier:	O Mother, Mother dear!

Here the reunited pair refused to fall into one another's arms, in spite of the roaring applause. They were not indeed encouraged to do so by the Master, whose strict ideas of propriety were reinforced by the even stricter moral code of his wife, felicitously christened 'Tin Ribs' by Alfred years before. Instead, the two young artists bowed awkwardly to their moved and applauding public.

They were replaced on the stage by a line of Irish Colleens singing improbably: 'We're dainty little Geishas and we come from old Japan.' Japan was indeed very fashionable then; and never out of fashion was Ireland, that dear homeland of all.

All the children, (three-quarters of them Orange to the backbone), sang most movingly, apostrophising their country to -

'Remember the days of old, ere her faithless sons betrayed her,
When Malachi (to them one of the more pronounceable prophets), wore the collar of gold,
That he won from the proud invader.'

And so it went on through 'Emerald Gems' and 'Red Branch Knights' that belonged utterly to these children. They knew they were Irish. They knew they were British. They knew they were Ulster. They had not the slightest difficulty in being all three, any more than a Cockney had in being a Southener, a Londoner, an Englishman and a Briton all at once. But some ancient Scots-Irish blood showed in their undoubted penchant for poems in Lallans like 'The Bairnies Cuddle Doon,' 'The Auld-Farrant Wean,' 'The Wee Humpie' and that richest of all versions of the well-known rhyme, 'Wee Willie Winkie.' It was a solo piece:

92

> 'Wee Willie Winkie rins through the toon,
> Upstairs and doonstairs in his nicht goon,
> Tirlin' at the window, cryin' at the lock,
> "Are the weans in their beds? It's past ten o'clock".'

- and so on and on in endless verses of familiar unfamiliarity in that liveliest of tongues.

Moving within his happy element, the Master rose to take his boys through their Physical Jerks with barbells. No Sergeant-Major in any Regiment of the great British Army had a more commanding presence, a more swelling chest, a sharper voice or a finer spray of saliva. Up jerked the boys, down jerked the boys, out, in, up, down, never, oh, never an error. It was not allowed. The Master's face relaxed into something approaching a smile at the successful completion of his Army's manoeuvres.

Mary had coached one Senior Girl in her Recitations and fully shared the nervous tension of the other Producers. Aggie did not let her down. The audience hung on the fine unbroken flow of, first, the charming fantastical and, second, the sentimental melancholy. The latter being so much more to the taste of the audience of the day, it was saved for the more important position. So Aggie started off with -

> 'Wynken, Blynken and Nod one night
> Set off in a wooden shoe,
> Sailed on a river of misty light
> Into a sea of dew ...'

and proceeded, emboldened by her first applause, to ensure with her second poem that there was not a dry eye in the house. In truth, she brought to her recitation a really touching quality that surprised even her youthful instructress.

> 'The little toy dog is covered with dust,
> But sturdy and staunch he stands.
> The little tin soldier is red with rust,
> And his musket moulds in his hands.
>
> Time was when the little toy dog was new
> And the soldier was passing fair.
> Ah! that was the time our Little Boy Blue
> Kissed them and put them there.

"Now, don't you go till I come," he said,
"And don't you make any noise."
And, toddling off to his trundle bed,
He dreamt of the pretty toys.

And, as he was dreaming, an angel song
Awakened our Little Boy Blue.
Oh! the years are many, the years are long,
But the little toy friends are true.

Ay! faithful to Little Boy Blue they stand,
Each in the same old place,
Awaiting the touch of a tiny hand,
The smile on a little face.

And they wonder, as waiting these long years through
In the dust of that little chair,
"What has become of our Little Boy Blue?"
Since he kissed them and put them there.'

The Master's dear love, those dozens and dozens of children out of his two hundred who formed the School Choir, now brought the Concert section of the evening to its close. Those great hobbledehoy lads, (the bare footed of them hidden in the middle of the back row) were well trained true tenors and basses, the big girls fruity altos, and both girls and little boys sweet fluting trebles. They made their concession to the secular world with a song Mary dearly loved although it both puzzled her and made her giggle. It was called 'Our old brown homestead,' and she used to wonder about this since she never knew anyone who had a homestead, let alone a brown one. She knew only people with houses, and those were whitewashed, pebble dashed, rough cast or of plain red brick. Her giggles came, you may guess, in the last verse, until familiarity soothed them away.

'Our old brown homestead reared its walls
From the wayside dust aloof,
Where the apple boughs could almost cast
Their fruitage on its roof.
The cherry tree so near it stood
That, when awake I've lain
In the lonesome night, I've heard the limbs
As they crackled 'gainst the pane.

The sweet-briar 'neath the window sill
Which the early birds made glad,
And the rose bush by the garden wall
Were all the flowers we had.
I've looked on many flowers since then,
Exotic, rich and rare,
That to other eyes were lovelier
But to me were not so fair.

We had a well, a deep old well,
Which was never, never dry,
And the cool drops from the mossy stone
Were falling constantly.
There ne'er was water half so sweet
As that which filled my cup,
Drawn from the well by the rude old sweep
Which my father's hand set up.'

In case anyone should think it impossible to follow this, the
four soaring parts launched immediately into their real love -
the hymns, songs, choruses, call them what you will - that they
learned from the Master's mission zeal. Earnest boys' faces,
glowing above their white, wide celluloid collars, showed nothing
but concentration and piety. 'There's not a Friend like the lowly
Jesus,' they rejoiced, 'No, not one. No, not one.' Only a cynic
like Mary would have had a glancing memory of the same pious
faces roaring by the river, safely out of the Master's ear shot,
'There's not a heart in a gravy ring, No, not one. No, not one.'
'Whosoever will,' they sang on, the girls' sweet voices over-
topping the other parts, and 'Wonderful words' and 'Work for
the night is coming.' 'What a friend we have in Jesus,' continued
the choir, now well into its Christian stride, 'Nothing but the
Blood' and 'Throw out the life line' and 'The Sweet Bye and
Bye.' They approached the end of their present religious recital.
'Blessed be the Fountain,' the girls sailed on. The boys were
hanging fire the tiniest bit for they had their big finish coming
in the chorus, when the girls would sing 'Whi ...' and, before
they got to '... ter' the boys would have to insert neatly,
'Whiter than the snow' So it went throughout the chorus,
earnestness and joy emanating from the sweating youngsters.
The long shining hair of the girls quivered with 'nerves' and
effort. 'Whiter than the Snow' went the boys again. And again,
'Whiter than the Snow'. 'Wash me in the blood of the Lamb,'
went the girls, 'And I shall be whiter than snow.'

Mary, staring with real affection at all those faces fixed on their earthly Master, marvelled at that pleasure and cheerfulness she saw, that faith and piety. She could now reconcile it completely with that other side of these dear children that she and she alone of the Staff knew - that to them parody was the best of all forms of entertainment - and that those sweet voices meant no disrespect whatever when they shouted in the loney, 'Wash me in the water that you washed your dirty daughter in and I shall be whiter than snow'!

The Concert successfully concluded, the evening moved to its dignified climax, the Prize Giving. There was a great bustling on the stage by Miss Waide and Miss Allen to tidy away any remains of Concert or tea. The side table was carefully stacked with the ready-prepared Books and Medals. The smaller table was clad now in a red chenille cover fringed with plush balls. Chairs were placed for the Wee Buddy and his Consort. The Master stood at the ready, Prize List in hand. A silence fell on the audience, a silence of anticipation.

Slowly and graciously, Mr McMeekin rose and, with a chivalry that turned the knife in the hearts of wives of lesser men, handed his wife before him and assisted her into her chair. A round of applause for the well intentioned little pair broke out spontaneously from the audience. When the Master considered that this had gone on long enough, he bent his most meaningful look on the public and silence fell.

With respect, the Master introduced - although he himself truly said he had no need to introduce - the mill owner to his people. Mr McMeekin rose suitably to the calling applause and, addressing himself specifically to the children and only incidentally to his workers, spoke to them kindly of the virtues of industry and obedience. The Master began to call over the names of those who had won prizes. There may have been a damn-your-eyes look on some secret, defiant faces that knew full well when the Roll was called up yonder, they wouldn't be there. Mrs McMeekin was indefatigably gracious to each small girl or tall lad receiving a book prize with one hand and a handshake with the other. This was always a muddling process, and some children took long to get over the humiliation of doing things the wrong way round.

Then came the medals. The Master had a careful system of marks throughout the year for the book prizes, but the medals were awarded for only two things - good attendance, and good conduct. Good attenders at school were going to be good time-

96

keepers at work, and fair was fair. Anyone was allowed to miss three days for a death in the immediate family circle without having his medal withheld. Naturally, anyone who missed a day for any other reason couldn't expect a medal, but even here generosity prevailed with absence of one, two or three days being rewarded with books of graded price. A silver medal went to every child with a year's unbroken attendance at school; a silver medal with gold centre to all with three years; a gold medal to those with five. The cheering for these pupils was tremendous, and many a new resolution was made by the parents of children who had drooped with coryza or 'the squinsy' when they might have been earning glory.

Last of all came the greatest gold medal of the Prize Giving - the Good Conduct Medal. Up came John Duncan, in fine dark suit and lace collar like Little Lord Fauntleroy, to receive it. John was a rarity, a Good Boy. He got into such a habit of getting the Good Conduct Medal that it really became quite a dis-incentive to naughty boys who, with no hope of winning it, ignored the medal and were happily mischievous.

All was over. The Master led three cheers for their generous benefactors, and conducted choir and standing audience in a performance of the Twenty Third Psalm to that great tune, Orlington. Naturally, the Wee Buddy and his wife did not sing, but their children joined kindly with everyone else in the magnificent music.

In a respectful silence, the audience continued standing until the Master had conducted their benefactors to their horseless carriage. Secure now in their upholstered splendour, they glided off into the night behind John Gibson's liveried back, while snowflakes continued to float past their windows.

Next morning came, the very last day of Term, devoted to tidying up after the Swarry, removing Christmas paper garlands and controlling children ready to be off on holiday. Mary was surprised and a little disturbed to receive a message from the Big Room, ordering her to present herself at once before the Master.

She could read nothing from his expressionless face as she came in from her class in the Low Gallery. The Master quietly motioned, directing her gaze to a group of silent, shawled women assembled outside in the chill December air.

'Go out to them,' he said.

Mary hesitated and then went to the porch, closing the Big Room door behind her. She looked wide eyed from one woman to another, seeking an explanation.

'One woman shuffled her bare feet uneasily on the cinders.'

'Yes?' she queried, gently.

There was a heavy silence. One woman shuffled her bare feet uneasily on the cinders. Then another, braver than the rest, spoke up. Soon Mary knew all. She felt aghast. These were the harridans of the night before. Beggsie had let the Wee Buddy know of their behaviour. They had every one been sacked on the spot.

But perhaps the Spirit of Christmas had been with the owner. He had offered them the possibility of being reconsidered for labour after they had apologised sufficently abjectly to the Monitress. They apologised. Mary flushed hot with shame. Tears stung behind her eyes. She felt a totally unreasonable guilt. As quickly as she could, she stammered an acceptance of the unwanted apologies and fled to safety in the Low Gallery.

She never again in all her life wished to see such an exercise of power. That incident stayed with her always.

Chapter 8

Throughout her teaching life, Mary found no place like school for entertainment. It was hard work. It was demanding and exhausting, but it never lacked humour of some sort. In those far-off days, pupils could and did arrive at any time of the year, from the babies whose mothers could at last get them into safety while they returned to work in the mill, to the often-much-older children who came with their parents, the scutchers, itinerant from mill to mill until all the flax was prepared for spinning into linen thread.

Most new pupils settled down easily after the first strange hours, but there were those who didn't. Mary realised that it was not fair to laugh at them, so they seldom saw her reaction to their plight. But the little souls struggling to cope with a strange and frightening environment produced smiles as well as tears. It was not too difficult to get them settled, if only their mothers were strong minded enough to put them gently inside the school room with children they knew, and leave them. In all Mary's career, only one mother persisted past all common sense in trying to stay seated with her baby on the infant form. All the coaxing and cajoling in the world couldn't get that mother to go home and leave her little May behind in this alien world. When she at last got to the stage of suggesting to Mary that she continue thus for several days, the youthful Monitress, left without another teacher near to help, had to summon up all her reserves of patience, firmness and bullying to get May's mother up off the form and out through the school room door, where she lingered for a long time in the hall way. Little May promptly forgot her mother and started to play with the infant boy beside her, still dressed, like most boys of his age, in petticoats.

One such petticoated boy Mary remembered for the rest of her life, for she was in charge of his class and therefore, theoretically, of him. It was his first day at school for William. He came falteringly down the cindered lane to the school, clinging to the hand of his older sister. Lily promptly left him when they reached the cassie and careered off to join her noisy comrades in their chasing game. Apparently William just stood and gazed at the screaming, romping, hurly-burly round him, decided that if this were school he didn't like it, and headed for home again. But in that little mind were already the seeds of an intelligence that were to grow successfully in later years, for he did not return by the footpath way where he would too easily be seen.

When the school bell sounded its assembly note, the classes, suddenly hushed, lined up in silence and began their ritual march into school by their proper doors. Chink! Chink! Chink! went the clapper of the handbell as the Master kept time for those marching feet on the rough cassie. Mary's Baby Infants came marching into the Low Gallery, with clumping clogs and boots or silent bare feet on the wooden boards. William's big sister was permitted to come in from her class to give Mary what were known as his 'pa-teek-lers' for the sacred Roll Book.

'Brother? What brother?' said Mary, her eyes roving rapidly over the fussing class searching for a strange face.

'Wullyum,' said the juvenile mitcher's sister, also searching for that little rosy countenance.

In a few moments, she and Mary had concluded that 'Wullyum' wasn't there. They looked at one another in consternation, one feeling as guilty as the other.

'Go and tell the Master, quick,' said Mary her heart sinking as she thought of the little Doagh River, the sluices and leats and mill dams, and, worst of all, the great wooden wheel turning in its bottomless pit of water by the scutch mill.

The Master came quickly in.

'Get after him and find him,' he said to Mary and Lily, and went to despatch senior boys to join in the search. The two girls rushed out by the porch door. Mary throwing directions to Lily over her shoulder.

'You take the loney home and I'll go up by the burn,' she shouted.

She took to her heels in the direction of the stepping stones that provided a rather longer but more interesting 'short-cut' to William's home. She ran like a two-year-old and there, sure enough, standing contemplating the brown peaty water that swirled by smooth stones and chattered over rough, was William.

Mary grabbed him by the petticoats in case he took to the water before she could speak to him.

101

'Now, now, William,' she said. 'You can't go in that dirty old water. You would spoil your lovely new boots. Aren't those just lovely boots? Where'd you get those nice boots?'

The infant Wullyum regarded his little buttoned boots seriously. Then he stared solemnly into Mary's grey eyes, on a level with his as she knelt by the river. He said nothing.

'Come on, Willie,' said Mary gently. 'Come on and we'll go back to school.'

'Naw,' said Wullyum. He stared across the river to the far bank where the stepping stones led to the hill at the back of Beggs's pub.

'You have to go to school, you know, Willie,' said Mary, still gently. 'You'll like it. You wait and see.'

'Naw,' said Wullyum.

Mary began to feel desperation rising inside her. He was her responsibility. How in heaven's name was he to be shifted from his intransigent position? Even physically it would be quite a feat for her. Wullyum was a sonsy boy. She decided to call in reinforcements. Still holding Willie's tails, she stood up and shouted in the direction of the loney.

'Li-ly!' she called. 'Li-ly!'

There was no answer, but in a moment she thought she heard feet pounding on the packed cinders. Sure enough, a red faced worried Lily came into view, her pig tails flying behind her, one boot lace undone, and a general air of dishevelment showing. Panting, she stopped by Mary and her brother, tiny sweat beads on her freckled nose. She would have hammered Willie if Mary hadn't been there, she was so relieved.

'Come you on this minnit,' she ordered. Wullyum looked up at them both from under his brows.

'Come on, Willie,' Mary tried again. 'You'll like school.'

The laconic Wullyum spoke.

'Ah wuz *at* school. Ah dinnae like it,' and he shut his baby mouth like a mantrap and turned to the burn.

'You weren't really at school,' said Mary, taking one baby hand and signalling with her eyebrows for Lily to take the other. 'You've never even seen the lovely beads and blocks and slates and dumbells and - and -' She ran out of inspiration.

'Ah dinnae like school,' said Wullyum unreasonably. His sister shook him by the arm she held. Letting her down like this, the pup.

'That'll do, Lily,' said Mary, '... and - and (inspiration flowed back) - Drill. You go Left! Right! Left! Right! like soldiers. And "About Turn" and "At the Double" and everything. It's lovely.'

102

She demonstrated with spirit. Wullyum's eyes were definitely showing interest.

'And "Quick March" every day - every half-hour, every day. And there's music, just like the Cogry Band. And you can march as much as you like.' This last was a definite stretching of solemn truth.

'Aw right,' said Wullyum at last. 'Ah'll come an' merch. But Ah'm daein nithin' else.' And with a girl holding each hand, the runaway Baby Infant came back to give school another try. The girls held their captive tightly, and as all three ran back towards the school, Willie's infant feet left the ground, and to his own pleasure he was swung, laughing and red faced, back to a friendlier place than that he had left a bare half-hour earlier.

Mary was often faced with the difficulties presented to new Infants by their bodily functions. Some babies were too shy to ask out, and presented her instead with a puddle on the floor. Some were so uninhibited that they might be typified by one baby boy who shall remain nameless for ever.

Halfway through his first morning at school, he stood up, all three feet of him, and announced, 'Ah want oot.'

Fair enough.

Mary told another boy to take him, in spite of the nameless one's reiterations that he knew where to go. The class went on with its Chart Reading. Bang! The door opened. Crash! Anon stood there red faced, bright eyed, desperate, trousers clutched round his knees.

'Gies a bitta paper,' he said.

Mary could cope easily with such little emergencies, for a natural upbringing with brothers and sisters on a farm make all life part of nature. But before leaving this subject that one could only hope to touch upon, so great are its ramifications, Mary's life as a Monitress would be but incompletely recounted if one were not to mention the Cautionary Tale of Tommy and his Mother.

When Tommy arrived at school one morning in early spring, he was, Mary considered, the very smallest child for his age she had ever seen. Apart from the fact that he was fine boned, with tiny hands and feet, he was at least a head shorter than the next smallest infant in the Low Gallery. He, too, was brought to school by an older sister, but unlike Wullyum, he settled down immediately and happily to making scribbles on his slate with a slate pencil. When this palled, he went on with his fellow infants

' "Gies a bitta paper," he said.'

to build wee houses of wooden blocks.

By the middle of the morning, however, all was not well. Mary noticed him crying silently to himself, the tears coursing slowly down his tiny face.

'D'you want out, Tommy?' Mary asked.

He brightened and nodded his head.

'Just a minute and I'll get Minnie,' she said and went over to the Big Room to borrow his sister from Miss Waide's Class. Infants to be initiated were allowed such help for one day.

Minnie came in cheerfully enough and departed with her little brother. In a few moments they returned and Tommy resumed his seat on the gallery steps. But the little face was still woebegone, and still the silent tears flowed.

'Did you not go out?' asked Mary.

Tommy nodded a tearful head.

'Well, you'd better go again,' said Mary and borrowed Minnie back.

Within a few moments, they returned as before, but Mary had learned that a thing well begun was not necessarily even half done. She held on to Minnie firmly and waited to see how Tommy would settle. He didn't. By now the little face was not just tearful but dirty, as various high-tide marks were left by the salt wash and his grubby fingers.

'Tommy, come here this minute,' said Mary, determined to have what Aunt Laetitia called 'No Nonsense.'

'Did you not go out with Minnie?'

Tommy drooped a shy and doeful head.

Mary was inspired.

'When you did go, did you *go*?'

Tommy shook his head sadly and burst into lamentable sobs.

'What does this mean?' said Mary, turning to the sister. 'Why did you not see that he *went*?'

'He *can't*,' said Minnie.

'What do you mean "can't"?' said Mary, suddenly seized by an ancient memory of a teacher of her own early schooldays who had smugly assured her there was no such word as 'can't.'

'He can't,' said Minnie again, shame faced.

Mary had sudden paralysis, struck by the thought that the child might have some terrible physical abnormality.

'Are you telling me he *can't*?' said she, in wonderment.

'No. My Ma sewed him up,' said Minnie, dropping her eyes modestly.

Dear heaven, sewed him up! Mary was inhibited by none of Aunt Laetitia's delicacy. She inspected Tommy and sure enough he was dressed in a one piece garment, a boy's jersey so long for his tiny frame that, stitched roughly at the crotch, it made a romper suit from which he would never emerge until he was unpicked. From the needlework box, Mary grabbed a pair of fine scissors.

'Now, you stand *dead still*,' she said to the pathetic sufferer, and in a few careful snips, he was released from both the rompers and the room. When he did at last return, he was not the only one who was relieved!

The place to which Tommy, Wullyum and all other children went was one of two closets built, as were all country conveniences, jutting out over the river so that they were permanent Water Closets. The mill owner's wife later discovered to her understandable horror that the same stream down river provided for her sanitation also, in the new-fangled bathroom of her home. Thereafter the position of the closets was moved from water to dry land, so that the cess pits were now a problem for the Independent Row and the school rather than for the mill owner's wife. Mary, too, could not help a sneaking feeling that it was even a marginal improvement for the children, who had been compelled also to wash in the river if the Master pronounced them unclean.

The teachers, too, had a little tarred shed abutting on the river. It was part of Sam Phillips's shed and had been tarred outside and whitewashed inside by him. Sam lived in a house in the Independent Row that joined on in a single line to the school and the scutch mill. Mrs Phillips's home was the cloak room for all teachers' appurtenances, and she provided further for their comfort by creating a luncheon room of her kitchen and giving them a good pot of strong tea. Mary loved Mrs Phillips, that same Mrs Phillips whose bonnet with jet wired beads had whiled away many a boring hour in church for Mary the child.

Hygiene was not, and could not be, a great feature of the early National School. It was, however, taught in School to Mary the Monitress for examination purposes. These had, as usual, no connection with everyday living. Instead, children were reliably informed by their parents that dirt, lice, manure, rotting flax and many other equally delightful concomitants of the rural scene were healthy.

One strange smell was associated only with school. It emanated from the piles of slates on window sills and in cupboards. Everyone began his school career on a slate. These were smaller and of a finer grain than roofing slates, and suitable scratches could be made on them with a round pencil also made of slate. When writing or ciphering were finished, Authority said that the slates were to be wiped clean. It was assumed by Authority that such wiping would take place in an ideal school, where each child had not just his own personal slate, but copious supplies of sponge and water as well.

Far from the truth was the real scene, where each child got the one handed to him fortuitously when the slates were given out. He had no sponge, although a few children of advanced parents did bring a little damp flannel with them daily in their strap or satchel. But the majority of Irish mankind used one of Nature's more convenient sources of water, and tens of thousands of spits landed daily on Irish slates to be wiped clean and dry by an equal number of Irish sleeves.

The slates had a blank reverse while the obverse was ruled from side to side with six equidistant lines. On these Infants learned to write. There was no such thing as printing. Later, an expert produced one original thought - that it must be difficult for children to proceed from cursive writing on slate or copy book to the printed page of the First Reader. The obvious fact that children already were proceeding happily from one to the other must have escaped the expert's notice, for the edict came forth from Authority that all Infants would now *print* their letters and words and proceed much later to the adult world of 'joined writing.' It seemed to Mary in her later years that all that happened as a result of the opinions of experts, especially of theorising inspectors, was that children learned neither to spell nor to write, neither to read nor to count. It was a sad day for her when the pendulum of the Three R's swung from the world of rote and copperplate to that other world which regarded accuracy and literacy as something actually bad for children. It was to be her hope that when teachers had fewer experts around, the pendulum might just possibly come to rest somewhere in the middle!

As Mary served her time, however, legible hand-writing was considered to be of the greatest importance, being on a par with the skill of reading. When one considers that many parents and all grandparents of these children could neither read nor write, it was not surprising that these crafts were held in such veneration. Penmanship was, in fact, a 'failing' subject in the King's Scholarship that would be the reward of any successful student at the end of five years' practical teaching. Indeed, such penmanship might be a young lad's only craft, but it would be sufficient to make a clerk of him in any of the local industries. Such a position was jealously sought for, being considered a cut above manual work. This was an amusing thought to Mary, as nothing could be more manual than penmanship. But a clerkship was important for the more worthwhile reason that it did offer greater opportunities for promotion, even in one case Mary knew, to eventual share in the ownership of mills.

Every thanks was due to that great educationist and philanthropist ever associated in Mary's mind with hand-writing - Vere Foster. An Irishman who happened to have been born in Denmark, he was possessed of a great fortune. This he devoted, as he devoted himself, to the service of the poor of Ireland in innumerable ways. From financing emigrants and even accompanying them to their new homes to see them settled, from saving all the poor he could from the rigours of the Great Famine, from rebuilding and repairing two thousand of Ireland's little National Schools, from bettering the lot of Irish teachers who were paid only one-third of an English teacher's salary - from all these large and successfully accomplished tasks he could come down to the very detail of the Irish schoolchild's daily requirements for learning. Thus he designed for them the beautiful copy books that bore his name. They were the best memorial an educationist could have had. To help ensure that his beloved children would become literate and thus help themselves, he gave a million copies of these beautiful books to schools, along with three thousand pounds every year in prizes for the best writers. Ireland has never acknowledged her debt to this magnificent man who really did give his life for her. Mary acknowledges it today with truest admiration.

The economical slates were, nevertheless, the surfaces on which every child's penmanship began. The six ruled lines showed the limits within which small letters stayed, or on which looped letters were cut. No infant seemed to object to doing little slanted strokes, straight down strokes, slants with curves attached or pot hooks. They were to him perhaps just part of the teacher's general madness. But on the same slate he could soon use these bits and pieces to tell the world that 'A little pot is soon hot.'

When he could write on his slate, he was ready to transfer from the easy slate, pencil and spit, to the Vere Foster pen, ink and copy book. Ireland was a country of pen-men, who were not always saintly but certainly had something about them of the scholarly.

Mary never could remember in later life just when she first

started to take a more-than-casual interest in the people round her. Incident after incident and character upon character piled up in a great heap of riches in her greedy mind so that she fed on them with satisfaction throughout her life. So many things were illustrative of the dual nature of her beloved fellow countrymen that she, like them, found herself with a double attitude of mind - a sharing in the immediate incident along with a mental pigeon-holing of the scene for future reference. As for her fellows' dual nature, the superstitious pagan dwelt inevitably inside the same carcase as the pietistic Ulsterman. And with his good business sense, the Ulsterman would admit it candidly. 'No, I'm not one bit superstitious, but there's no sense in taking any chances.' It was an attitude of mind that made for a fine feeling of security.

One day, Mary was swinging along the footpath to Ballyclare. This was the pleasant summer way of approaching the town from her home, through fields and over stiles to the Thorn Dyke where one could still see blooming the white-pearled blackthorns planted aeons ago to mark the Eastern limit of Lord Donegall's estate. Before her she saw a shawled woman also evidently going to town by the footpath way. Mary hastened her step a little to catch her up, but the young woman reached the halfway house, Mellons' farm, before her. Grannie Mellon leaned over her half-door where pink roses nodded daintily to the white-wash on the walls. Mary could hear the young woman greet Grannie cheerfully.

'Lovely day that,' she said.

'Lovely, just lovely, Sarah.' said Grannie. 'That's a right wee lump ye have there.'

The 'right wee lump' proved to be a new baby, nestling in the folds of the carrying-shawl. (One could not have found half-a-dozen perambulators in as many townlands). Mary turned the corner of the house in time to see the young mother gently move the shawl to show the small red, sleeping face, one hand clutching a woolly fold displaying tiny, infant nails.

'He *is* a right lump,' agreed the mother. 'I'm glad to change round,' and she proceeded to re-arrange shawl and infant in her other arm.

'Here's Mary,' said Grannie. 'Come on in, the pair of you and get a drink of buttermilk I churned this very morning. It's a brave step still.' Mary smiled her thanks and waited for Sarah to precede her. She was pulled up sharply by Grannie Mellon's next speech.

'Are ye churched yet, Sarah, all right?'

109

'Mellons' little homestead was one of Mary's favourite calling-houses.'

'I am not,' said the dark young mother. 'Sure a chair here'll do me grand but.'

And so Mary passed into the Mellon kitchen for her delicious acid milk, while the 'unchurched' mother sat sipping placidly on a wooden chair outside the home into which she would have brought 'Bad Luck.'

Mellons' little homestead was one of Mary's favourite calling houses. It was completely typical of its kind. Such small houses were of one storey, thatched and whitewashed. If at all possible the thatch was of best wheat straw, but oat straw, heather, rushes and even sods could provide a waterproof covering for the rafters. In Mellons' cottage, the ridge of the roof was made of a great tree trunk, roughly trimmed but still visible to Mary's naked eye. It rested on top of each room-wall throughout the length of the cottage, carrying the rafters with their straw covering that kept the house snug in winter and cool in summer. A cottage was just such a home, with a back room and a front room. Occasionally, there would be only one room with a half-loft above reached by a ladder. A grander cottage had back and front rooms with a scullery added to the side. A farmhouse like Mellons' had several rooms and, from without, seemed a very large house indeed because of the outhouses joined on to it in a long unbroken line.

It was customary to have no back door. There was just The Door. It was customary to have a rough yard in front of the door. It was customary to have the manure heap on the other side of the yard in full view of the house. It was customary to make no provision for human sanitation. Water for drinking was drawn from a spring well, and humans and animals shared the group of stable or byre for natural functions. Mellons' was more up-to-date, having a closet in the yard, and a flagged rather than an earthen floor in the kitchen. The other rooms of this commodious home had floors of scrubbed deal planking.

The heart of the house in every sense was the kitchen. A door on either side of it led to a parlour-cum-bedroom on one side and to two communicating bedrooms on the other. All was perfectly clean and neat. The open fire burned sticks and turf on the broad hearth-stone. On either side of the fire was built a little shelf called a hob. On one hob sat the three-legged black pot that could be hooked on to a moving crane and swung out over the fire for boiling water, potatoes, porridge or anything else needing such a useful utensil.

On the other hob sat the big black kettle that could similarly

111

be swung on the crane. Beside the hearth stone on the left sat the oven pot in which bread was baked. On convenient hooks hung the frying pan and the griddle. All the vessels were made of heavy black cast iron. Grannie's long steel tongs and poker leaned against the steel fender that kept unauthorised persons from the fierce heat. 'Erin-go-Bragh' said the fender, shining from emery paper. Mary could read it easily among its scrolls of shamrocks. Beside the mantelpiece hung another object that might have said 'Beware!' This was the tawse, a leather strap with one end fringed as though by a Sioux Indian. The tawse kept law and order in every humble home. A flustered mother baking on a swinging griddle over the fierce heat of the fire with a baby in its wooden cradle and several others in various stages of crawling, walking and interfering, needed a handy, stinging, yet harmless instrument of justice. Who is to say that many did not, in later life, even look back on the tawse with a degree of affection?

At right angles to one hob was a settle bed. This was in appearance a box like seat as long as a sofa, with a high wooden back to keep off draughts. At night the box, which had provided a hard but comfortable and warm seat for several persons, was unlatched and opened down to floor level on hinges so as to make a wide wooden box with no lid. It contained a chaff or feather bed, with pillows and coverings for night time. It could sleep two adults or three children by the warm fire.

Against the wall opposite to the fireplace stood a tall, broad wooden dresser, with open shelves above two drawers and with two cupboards underneath them. The open shelves had nails in their edges so that a row of cups, tins and mugs hung before each shelf. At the backs of the shelves were ranged the larger plates, while in front of these were the smaller plates and saucers in piles, the striped and speckled bowls, the 'good' cups, the cream ewers and the milk jugs.

In one of the drawers, Grannie Mellon kept the knives and forks and spoons. In the other she had a wonderful agglomeration of kitchen necessities from a basting spoon to a corkscrew - the scissors, pieces of carefully saved twine, a tea strainer, the matches, Grannie's present bit of knitting on its needles, neatly folded brown paper, a card of plain pins, a little box of hairpins, a length of elastic, buttons, pieces of tape - the variety was endless.

In the cupboards underneath were, on the top shelf, the baking things; on the bottom shelf, the extra pot, the tea drawer, the egg saucepan and a box of cleaning stuffs helping to flavour all. The bake board hung from a nail in the side of the dresser, but the bake bowl of yellow glaze, the wee sharp knife and the goose wing all lived in the top shelf. The cleaning things in their box in the bottom shelf were Bath Brick for cleaning knives on a knife board, 'Monkey Brand' scouring powder, black lead and emery paper for a gleaming fireside, wax polish for the mahogany and horsehair furniture in Grannie's parlour-bedroom, starch and blue bag, and brass polish for the horse brasses and mantel rail.

To the other side of the great wide fire, fornenst the settle bed, was a wooden armchair with a cushion - Granda's seat - behind which was a large wall cupboard. In this stayed the groceries and stores in the top half, with larger everyday necessities like the bags of potatoes, flour and oatmeal in the bottom. A little table at the back window held cool brown crocks of buttermilk, sweet milk, and spring water. That back window sill was, like the front sill, frilled with white curtains and filled to overflowing with geraniums and the Bells of Ireland in pots, old tins and broken down saucepans. Room was left on the front sill for the paraffin lamp, its wick and globe cleaned daily, which gave the family light by night. The big table with its large quota of scrubbed-to-whiteness wooden chairs and stools for the family completed the larger furnishings.

On the mantelpiece stood the home's one clock, a dignified wooden timepiece with a good sense of its own importance. A fancy tin flanked it on either side, one holding the tea, the other odd coppers and silver - Grannie's savings from her housekeeping money for her large brood. Savings and tea were in turn guarded by delft dogs of strange pedigree. The red votive lamp by its sacred picture burned ever steadily. But the strange dual quality of the Irish mind found no conflict between the Saint Brigid's cross of rushes hung from a nail on the wall and the strong plaited 'churn' made from the last stalks of the past year's harvest hanging over the door as a fertility symbol, an offering to the old gods of the dark past.

Seated in Grannie Mellon's kitchen supping buttermilk, Mary reflected gloomily that she had nothing for the baby's handsel.

Neighbours and friends always brought gifts to a new-born child, the most popular being a silver coin. It was believed that if the tiny hand clutched this tightly, the child would live to be prosperous. If he let the coin fall, he was sure to be a spendthrift. Handselling was not confined to a new baby but applied to a new anything, especially to clothes, and very especially to

113

children's clothes. A penny or even a proud shilling would be slipped into the pocket of a new coat with the immemorial phrase:

> 'Health to wear,
> Strength to tear,
> And plenty of money to buy ye mair!'

Also for luck, the arm of coat and child would be nipped with, 'Good luck to you. That's a nice piece of stuff;' for nipping or pinching was also lucky.

The new baby was, however, guarded against other more immediate dangers than that of being a spendthrift. Everybody knew that the fairies could use nail parings and hair clippings to bring anyone under their spell. So the baby's nails and hair would not be cut until it was sometimes as much as a year old, by which time the fairies would have lost interest and concentrated on some less fortunate baby whose mother and friends might not know how to protect it. A baby with cut nails would grow up to be 'light-fingered' at the very least. The cutting of even adult nails was a ceremonial rite. Every clipping was carefully burnt, and nails must *never* be cut on a Sunday or the owner would come under a curse.

> 'Better the man had never been born
> Than he who his nails on a Sunday shorn.'

It was quite difficult for people to be sure of the right day for any activity. Sunday was never customary for anything except worship - witness the 'Man in the Moon' who 'Came down too soon, For gathering sticks on a Sunday!' Friday was well-known to be the most unpropitious day of the week for any undertaking, but especially for travelling, and no-one with sense moved house on a Saturday.

> 'A Saturday flit
> Is a short sit.'

It left few days to be getting on with necessary jobs at times, Wednesday also being unpropitious for business, moving house or travel, for Wednesday was one of the fairies' party days when they had a real get-together and wanted no mortals in their way.

It was not possible to arrange the day of a child's entry into the world. Nevertheless its future was decided for it by this involuntary act.

> 'Monday's child is fair of face,
> Tuesday's child is full of grace,
> Wednesday's child is born to woe,
> Thursday's child has far to go,
> Friday's child is loving and giving,
> Saturday's child works hard for a living.
> But the child that is born on the Sabbath day
> Is bonny and blithe and good and gay.'

Having protected her baby from nail and hair cutting, the young mother now had only to guard against its being overly praised (jealous fairies again), or of seeing its own reflection in a mirror. Everyone knew that mirrors carried more than their fair share of fortune. They bore Hallowe'en apparitions: they had a life within themselves, so they were covered up when there was a death in the house; and nothing could expiate the seven years' ill luck brought down by the other-world side of the mirror on the miscreant who broke it.

Less other-worldly but just as powerful as the mirrors were the birds. Some called the Willie-Wag-Tail the Divil's Bird as it had strong mystical powers, mostly for evil. If it lit upon a window sill tapping the pane, it was calling away the spirit of someone ill in the house. It had to do this for three mornings in succession, however, as all luck, good or bad, was ruled by the mystic three.

The robins and the swallows, on the other hand, brought nothing but good fortune to the house and must never be harmed. The cuckoo when first heard had high magical powers. You had to hold the little finger of the right hand to your lips (never the left), and spit over it, and wish. Then if you looked on the ground and found a hair, it was a sure sign that you would comb your own hair to a very old age. You could also receive guidance from the spring bird concerning your farming year.

> 'If cuckoo sits on a bare thorn,
> Sell your cow and buy your corn.
> If cuckoo sits on a sweet green bough,
> Sell your corn and buy a cow.'

The magpie was, however, the most powerful bird of all, going about in ones, twos, threes and so on, carrying good or bad luck to this or that person on the way.

> 'One for sorrow,
> Two for mirth,
> Three, a wedding,
> Four, a birth,
> Five, silver,
> Six, gold,
> Seven, a story never to be told.'

The trees on whose 'sweet green bough' the birds rested had their own powers. No one would ever cut a fairy thorn growing all alone in the middle of an arable field. The careful farmer would plough and sow and harvest uncomfortably round the tree rather than disturb the fairies. Most powerful of the trees were the may (hawthorn), the hazel, the yew and the rowan. The hazel could find water in the hands of a diviner and protect against witchcraft; the yew could poison and could bring death into the home by magic as well; whilst every house could be protected against dark principalities and powers by a bunch of rowan hung over the door and indeed over the baby's cradle and over the churn in the homes of (no, not superstitious) canny people. And if you caught it in time, nearly any spell could be broken and ill fortune chased away (say, after spilling salt or walking under a ladder) by saying quickly, 'Good luck to me - bad luck to you' and giving a good spit. The spit was part of nearly every rite, superstition or freit. ('Never follow freits or freits will follow you,' said one old woman to Mary most seriously), and the spit in the clasped hand sealed a bargain as surely as a fasting spittle cured 'wild-fire' or herpes.

Far beyond the power of birds or trees was the Woman Fairy herself, the Banshee. Local people said quite often that they had heard her wailing, but nobody ever seemed to hear her in time. She announced the Angel of Death, but her alleged keening was invariably recalled only after a death had taken place. Mary didn't believe them.

And anyhow, didn't the Banshee only announce an imminent death to one of the Ancient Families, to one of which Mary herself had the honour to belong?

Chapter 9

The year was nineteen hundred and five. Mary came home from school. She threw her books down on the dining room table where her homework was to be done. She was dusty and tired. It was only the first day of May and already the weather was unseasonably hot. She took off her clothes, washed lightly and put on a too short, faded cotton frock. As she straightened her hair before the dressing table mirror she stopped, hands still to her head. Surely that was the sound of singing?

Of course! the First of May! Why hadn't she thought of it? The singing must be coming from the May Queen and her retinue approaching the Bridge House, after serenading the cottagers who lived at the foot of the back lane. Shoving one of the sash windows up from the bottom, Mary leaned out over the leaded bay of the drawing room. Sure enough, the Queen's entourage was already entering by the garden gate. Her weariness forgotten, Mary flew downstairs to open the hall door. Little Sister was racing for it too along the hallway from the back regions, a jam piece in her hand.

The May Queen stood on the top-most of the three steps, her courtiers and hangers-on ranged befittingly on lower levels. With apparent unanimity they burst into song.

> 'To be the Queen o' the May,
> To be the Queen o' the May,
> To welcome (Maggie Murphy,
> Murphy, Murphy),
> To welcome (Maggie Murphy)
> To be the Queen o' the May,
>
> Heigh-ho, Bra-vo
> Our Queen one,

Our Queen one,
Our Queen one,
Heigh-ho, Bra-vo
Our Queen one.'

'Our Queen one' was gowned in lace curtains which provided
over-dress, train and veil. She was crowned with a chaplet of
Mayflowers (kingcups), and carried a large bouquet of the same
golden blossoms. Her numerous courtiers, both boys and girls,
were dressed as well as they could muster costumes, and carried
ash plants, hawthorn blossoms and Mayflowers. One boy had a
blackened face. Another rather smaller boy had charge of the
Royal Coach, an old go-chair camouflaged with a patchwork
quilt and decorated with buttercups and daisies. The May Queen
was pushed from house to house before dismounting graciously
to greet each of her loyal subjects. Lustily the court roared away.

'The darkie said he would marry her,
Marry her, marry her,
The darkie said he would marry her
Because she was the Queen.
Because she was the Queen,
The darkie said he would marry her
Because she was the Queen.'

The 'darkie' stepped forward and bowed. Then Her Gracious
Majesty performed courteously as the singing continued.

'Our Queen can birl her leg,
Birl her leg, birl her leg.
Our Queen can birl her leg,
Birl her leg.'

This balletic performance was followed by the first hint of
any commercial interest in the rite.

'Our Queen can eat a curr'nt loaf,
Eat a curmn't loaf, eat a curr'nt loaf,
Our Queen can eat a curr'nt loaf,
Eat a curmn't loaf.

Lady, you have gold and silver.
Lady, you have a house and land.
Lady, you have ships on the ocean.
All I want is a penny if you can.'

As Aunt Laetitia had no currant loaf, Mary went indoors again to fetch a penny for the collecting box, from the riches of which gathered store all the court would regale themselves on lemonade, sweeties and shop buns.

Her May Majesty withdrew again within her chariot and the court progressed on its way.

> 'To be the Queen o' the May,
> To be the Queen o' the May ...'

Their song melted into the distance while their flowers and flounces drooped just a little more in the hot sun, though their energy continued unabated.

Mary never tired of listening to the scraps of songs, responses, words, sayings and riddles of her young charges. Often and often when they were not aware of being overheard, they provided her with more and more material for her collection of Ulster children's lore. Just as the set seasons for games happened without any apparent guidance, so the songs, rhymes and sayings came from nowhere to be handed down to the next generation, also apparently from thin air. They certainly had justification for their high favoured but most secret chant.

> 'Old J.P. is a very good man,
> He goes to the Meetin' on Sunday
> To pray to God to give him strength
> To bate the weans on Monday.'

Another song-for-the-fun-of-it was about that rare phenomenon, the policeman. Most of the pupils had never seen one, but that did not prevent their describing him.

> 'I wisht I was a bobby
> Dressed in bobby's clo'es,
> With a big tall hat
> An' a belly full o' fat
> And an Indian rubber nose.'

Yet another was the immortal quatrain,

> 'Dan, Dan, the funny wee man,
> Washed his face in the frying pan.
> He combed his hair with the donkey's tail
> And scratched his belly with his big toe nail.'

Any song with such reference to the human person was sure of a 'Belly' laugh every time, even to the puerile:

> 'Oh, my finger,
> Oh, my thumb,
> Oh, my belly,
> Oh, my bum!'

or the crude:

> 'Mary Ann Magee,
> She let a fartin flee,
> She roasted it,
> An' toasted it,
> An' took it to her tea.'

and the rude:

> 'Queen, Queen Caroline,
> Dipped her nose in turpentine
> Turpentine will make it shine,
> Queen, Queen Caroline.'

As with their songs and rhymes, the children's riddles ranged from the charming to the shocking. There was always a new intake of children to be taken in. The seniors lost little time initiating the juniors.

'Answer me this:

> "The Queen of Morocco
> She sent to Queen Anne
> A bottomless vessel
> To put flesh and blood in?" '
> (A Ring)

'Where was Moses when the light went out?' (This had three acceptable answers: 'In the dark,' 'Under the bed lookin' for matches,' 'In his waistcoat pocket feeling for a Vesta.')
'What goes up the chimney down but can't go down the chimney up?' (An umbrella.)
'What runs but can't walk?' (The burn.)
'What gets bigger the more you take away?' (A hole.)
'Which is heavier, a pound of feathers or a pound of lead?'

(Ha! Ha! both the same!)

'When is a cow not a cow?' (When it is turned into a field.)

'Should you say "The yolk of an egg is white or the yolk of an egg are white?" ' (Catch riddle.)

> 'Little Nanny Etticoat
> In a white petticoat
> And a red rose,
> The longer she stands,
> The shorter she grows.' (A candle.)

> 'Riddle-me, Riddle-me, Randy-o,
> My father gave me seed to sow.
> The seed was black and the ground was white,
> Riddle-me, Riddle-me, Randy-o.' (Black writing on white paper.)

'What walks on four legs in the morning, two legs at mid-day and three legs in the evening?' (A man in his lifetime.)

'If a herrin' an' a half cost three ha-pence, how many apples in a barrel of grapes?' (Nonsense riddle.)

And so the stream of classics went on by the dozen, always drawing nearer and nearer to the local and the vulgar.

'Why did Sandy Row?' (To let Donegall Pass.)

'What goes up the water and down the water and never touches the water?' (An egg in a duck's ass.)

'Why does Queen Victoria wear red, white and blue lastic?' (To keep her drawers up!)

Screams of childish laughter greeted such sallies, and were echoed in the catch phrases.

'Say this as quick as you can - "Polish it in the corner" ' or "I chased a bug around the room",' or 'After every line you say "just like me".' The willing victim consenting -

> 'I went down a dark, dark road,' (Just like me.)
> 'And I went into an old dark house,' (Just like me.)
>   etc., etc.
> 'And there I saw a big black billy goat,' (Just like me.)

or

> 'Punch and Judy ran a race.
> Judy stopped to tie her lace.
> Who won?'

and on the answer 'Punch,' a vigorous blow was delivered on invitation. The correct answers to any of these catchers gave the questioner the right to administer punishment, as for example:

> 'James and John and Hammeron
> Went into the sea to bathe.
> James and John were drownded dead.
> Who do you think was saved?'

or

> 'Adam and Eve and Nipme
> Went out in a boat to sea.
> Adam and Eve were drownded dead.
> Which of the three was saved?'

If, by any unlikely chance, the children fell silent, one of their number soon got the fun going again by announcing, 'Silence in the pig market while the pigs say their prayers!' This might very well be the signal for starting a Counting Rhyme for choosing the players in a game. The Counting Rhymes were full of interest, vitality and excellent opportunities for quick brains to cheat, for one and all had to make certain that the right (or wrong) people were 'put out.'

> 'Our little Jinny
> Had a nice clean pinny.
> Guess what colour it was?'
> Answer: (say) Blue
> 'B-L-U-E spells Blue and Q-U-T spells Out.'

> 'One, two, three, four, five, six, seven,
> All good children go to heaven,
> When they die, their sins forgiven.
> One, two, three, four, five, six, seven.'

> 'Eeny meeny miney mo,
> Catch a nigger by the toe.
> If he hollers let him go,
> Eeny meeny miney mo.'

or

> 'Eeny meeny miney mo,

122

Set the baby on the po,
When he's done, clean his bum,
Eeny meeny miney mo.'

or

'Eeny meeny hippersy Dick,
Delia, Dahlia, Dominick,
Each, peach, pear, plum,
Out goes my chum.'

To the simple manners of 'Excuse me,' it was fashionable to exclaim, 'You're quite excusable, but your fault's none the less.' Similarly to 'What?' the answer came with lightning speed. 'Stick your head in the porridge-pot and don't call me "What." '

If anyone continued trying to make an April Fool of a friend after twelve o'clock noon, he was smartly told:

'April Fool is past and gone,
You're the fool for carryin' on.
Three potatoes in the pot,
You're the fool and I'm not.'

Again, you could very often take in your friends with the simple question, 'Did you ever hear the story about the two wells?'
'No. What is it?'
'Well, well!'
To someone who left the door open after him, one was entitled to shout, 'Were you born in a field with the gate open?'
To the ordinary, one would think, question, 'What time is it?' the unenlightening answer would come:
'The same time as yesterday only a day farder on.'
'Where's the teacher?' (In her skin.)
A pupil who did not retort was reported as taking 'all insults as compliments!'
On all school books at one time or other would be found the inscription of the lad who was just beginning to find his feet as an individual:
'Lennox Dugan, Bridge House, Doagh, County Antrim, Ireland, Europe, The World, The Universe.'
This was usually in handwriting that the Master would not have called penmanship, as adolescents struggled in yet another way to grow up and be 'different.' The book might be further

mutilated with such puerilities as:

> 'If this book should chance to roam,
> Box its ears and send it home
> To .etc.'

Tongue twisters were always in fashion and many an unlucky child was compelled by older pupils to attempt to say them at speed.

'Around the ragged rocks the ragged rascals ran,' or

'She sells sea-shells by the sea-shore,' or

'Peter Piper picked a peck of pickled pepper off a pewter plate,' or

'Three gray geese in a green field grazing. Gray were the geese and green was the grazing.'

All remarks to playground fellows were not as lovable as:

> 'Roses are red,
> Violets are blue,
> Sugar is sweet,
> And so are you.'

Faintly, in the distance from time to time, Mary could hear a less agreeable chant directed at some unfortunate none-too-clean child.

> 'I think, I think,
> I smell a stink.
> I think, I think
> It's . . . . . . YOU!'

Or its variant,

> 'Ink, pink, pen and ink,
> Eetel, Eitel, Stottel, STINK!'

Of even greater interest to Mary were the games the children played before morning school and at lunch time. There were no 'organised games,' as the last thing the children wanted or needed was an organiser. Their own natural leaders were sufficient for them. When the half-past-twelve bell went, leaving them free until one o'clock, the children marched sedately to the outer doors and then burst into mad whoops and even madder races to nowhere. Free! Free! They were Free!

In no time at all pieces were eaten and water drunk from the communal tin and bucket in the porch. Older girls went off, arms twined round one another's waists, to saunter sedately up by the burn, over the stepping-stones to Burnside village, down the hill again to the Independent Loney and so back to school, having exchanged pleasant gossip and exciting confidences on the way.

The senior boys devoted themselves to their real passion, football. They did not always have a ball, but could bring from home rags of cloth or sheets of newspaper. Either of these could be wrapped and tied tightly in ball shape and kicked about until they disintegrated or flew into the river below, from which there was no possible throw-in. But sure the ball cost nothing and could be easily replaced!

Younger boys and girls played freely together. The muscle stretching and balance of hopscotch appealed to one as much as the other. So, too, they played Blind Man's Buff together with everyone rushing out of the blind man's reach and then creeping up behind to touch him, before dashing away again out of danger. The giddy blind man groped and darted here and there, and soon there was sure to be someone putting himself pretty deliberately in a position to be caught in order to become the next blind man.

Equally popular was 'Drop the Handkerchief.' A large ring of children hunkered down on the cassie, while one child with a handkerchief or piece of paper walked behind the seated children. Suddenly the dropper would let fall the handkerchief behind a squatting figure and scamper away, this time dashing in and out of the circle, encompassing a body here and there, twisting and turning like a raised hare. The dropee had to follow every twist and turn correctly while trying to catch the dropper, who tried to take his follower's empty place. If the dropper wasn't caught, the dropee took his place instead, and so the endless game went on until the children tired of it and moved to something else.

It might be 'Here are the Robbers coming through,' which had strange overtones of another far-off game. Two children formed an archway with upraised arms. The long line of players passed through singing, and every now and then the arch would descend to imprison a robber. The prisoner was then given a whispered choice of 'oranges or lemons,' and having made his choice, would go behind his new leader clasping him round the waist. In this way grew two long lines of oranges and lemons, who eventually had a tug-of-war over a set mark to decide the conquerors, and all the time the pleasant old tune and strange old words went on:

'Here are the robbers coming through,
Coming through, coming through,
Here are the robbers coming through,
My fair ladye.

'What did the robbers do on you,
Do on you, do on you?
What did the robbers do on you,
My fair ladye?

'They broke my watch and stole my chain,
Stole my chain, stole my chain,
They broke my watch and stole my chain,
My fair ladye.'

The pathetically beautiful 'Green Gravel' was quite Mary's favourite, as she listened to the childish voices unfolding some now-forgotten tragic tale, re-enacting it as they slowly circled.

'Green Gravel, Green Gravel,
Your grass is so green.
You're the fairest young damsel
That ever was seen.

'Green Gravel, Green Gravel,
Your true lover's dead,
And I've sent you a letter
To turn round your head.

'I washed her, I dried her,
And I rolled her in silk,
And I wrote down her name
With a glass pen and ink.'

'Green Gravel' always had to be a girl. No 'true lover' ever appeared in the game. 'Green Gravel' stood alone in the heart of the slow circle until two other girls came to attend upon her and support the drooping figure, while the circling children about-turned and continued to circle with mournful sweet notes.

Was it true what they said, that 'Green Gravel' was Ireland and Parnell her 'true lover?' Mary didn't believe a word of it. It was much, much older than that. Did not she herself as a tiny child have a recollection of that one name 'Parnell,' as her parents discussed his death with saddened faces? It was much older than Mary. Of that she was quite sure.

Could it be Robert Emmet? Mary toyed with this thought, for Emmet was one of the few real heroes of Ireland and a figure of genuine rather than manufactured idealism. But Mary so disliked that stupid creature, Sara Curran, who, having been loved by a hero and having had a most beautiful song written for her, (often sung by Little Sister in her rich, moving contralto), promptly married somebody else. How *could* she? After this, mark you -

> 'She is far from the land
> Where her young hero sleeps,
> And lovers around her are sighing:
> But coldly she turns
> From their gaze and weeps,
> For her heart in his grave is lying.'

So Mary put this thought of Emmet from her, for she wouldn't let Sara be 'Green Gravel.' Thomas Moore, Emmet's friend, had urged his listeners to make a grave for her, and with this sentiment Mary was in hearty agreement. Well, well, it was all over a long time now. It had all happened in Granpa Neal's day. And, indeed, 'Green Gravel' might be much, much older than even Granpa Neal.

A sudden change of mood not unknown to young ladies would send them helter-skelter to their ball games, only to return quickly to the ring again as they heard the clarion call:

> 'Gather in, gather in,
> For a big tiggin' ring,
> If you don't come now,
> You'll not get in!' (Repeated as necessary)

Two favourite ring games had a little in common, but obviously were based on two different long forgotten tales. Both involved the persons in the middle going in and out beneath the arched arms of the ring but here the resemblance ended. Any counting game could find first the person to be It. The 'It' was the one in the middle who then would, by rhyme, choose a partner, automatically to become the next 'It.'

127

'In and out those dusty bluebells,
In and out those dusty bluebells,
In and out those dusty bluebells,
I'll be your master.'

Then 'It' stopped behind the chosen partner while all sang
and 'It' acted:

'Tapper, apper, apper on the left-hand shoulder,
Tapper, apper, apper on the left-hand shoulder,
Tapper, apper, apper on the left-hand shoulder,
I'll be your master.'

The chosen partner falling in behind 'It' and clasping her
round the waist, they proceeded in and out by the arches to:

'Follow me to Londonderry,
Follow me to Londonderry,
Follow me to Londonderry,
I'll be your master.'

The other ring game that took players in and out through the
arches of the ring had a somewhat similar pattern but a completely different tune. The 'business' followed exactly the words
of the song, with much waving, finger wagging and hand-shaking
before they 'parted' to enable the deserted lover to choose a
new mate.

'Out and in the windows,
Out and in the windows,
Out and in the windows,
As you have done before.

'Stand and face your lover,
Stand and face your lover,
Stand and face your lover,
As you have done before.

'Follow me to Dublin,
Follow me to Dublin, etc.

'Now we are married,
Now we are married, etc.

128

'I'll tell the bobbies,
I'll tell the bobbies, etc.

'Now we are parted,
Now we are parted, etc.

Fresh young voices could change instantly from songs to
'Pussy in the four corners.' Here, four girls made the four
corners of a square, with a fifth girl foot-loose in the middle.
While the 'Pussies' called 'Puss! Puss!' to one another, urging a
swapping about of corners, the fifth Pussy kept watch on all
four, trying always to dash successfully into an empty place.
While one group played this, the Babies in another corner of the
playground would be falling about happily as posies:

'Ringa, ringa, rosies,
A pottle, a pottle o' posies,
Husha! Husha!
We all fall down.'

There were three delightful rhymes that all had the same
object of play, that is to say, all started off with a senior pupil
swinging a baby infant gently to and fro, from side to side, and
then swinging the child in a huge upward arc on the last word. It
was by no means uncommon to see adults play these games
with screaming but delighted children who kept saying, 'Again!
Again!' after each dizzy, satisfying flight.

'Honey pots, honey pots, all in a row,
Twenty-five shillings wherever you go,
And A-W-A-Y!'

'Bluebells, Cockleshells,
Eevy, ivy, O-V-E-R-H-E-A-D!'

'Swing a bucket of water,
For a lady's daughter,
One in a rush,
Two in a bush,
Three to be off and A-W-A-Y!'

There were games with balls, with stones, with marbles, with
ropes. The skipping games had probably the finest words and
music. If a skipper skipped by herself - for skippers were always

'The skipping games had probably the finest words and music.'

girls - she could play little but 'Salt, Mustard, Cayenne Pepper,' the elegant slow pavane of 'Salt' reaching a hot coranto with the condiments as they progressed to the foot-entangling 'Pepper.' But with the long rope and a turner at either end, there were many variations. The running in and out while the rope was turning was quite a feat.

> 'Two little dicky-birds sat upon a wall,
> The one called Peter, the other called Paul.
> Fly away Peter. Fly away Paul.
> Come back Peter. Come back Paul.'

The places for stage business in this game were obvious, but with other skipping games the words often provided only a chanting in rhythm allied to a blush-making exposé.

> 'The wind, the wind, the wind blew high,
> The rain came scattering from the sky.
> Down came (Nelly) dressed in silk,
> A rose at her breast and a can of milk.
> "Oh," said (Nelly), "do you want a drink of this?"
> "No," said (Johnny), "I'd rather have a kiss." '

A more difficult variant on plain skipping involved the dropping and picking up again of a pebble representing a 'letter' in:

> 'Early in the morning at eight o'clock,
> You can hear the postman's knock.
> Postman, Postman, drop your letter.
> Postman, Postman, pick it up.'

Skipping was also used for fortune-telling by spelling names, or at least giving initials from the alphabet. Kind friends at the turning ends could always ensure that the skipper tripped up at the right boy's initials!

> 'Apple jelly, jam tart,
> Tell me the name of your sweetheart.
> A. B. C. . . . . .'

or

> 'Apply, apply, apply within,
> A woman put out for drinking gin!
> A. B. C. . . . . .'

Having acquired a prospective husband, the skipper would now be informed in the same way about her wedding dress.

'Silk, satin,
Velvet, cotton,
Muslin, rags.'

Mary noticed that you could always take a conceited girl down a peg or two by giving your little tug on the rope at 'rags.'

Further, you could find out your future social position using the same rhyme in either one of two ways - by using the magic of the skipping rope or by counting your buttons.

'Tinker, tailor,
Soldier, sailor,
Rich man, poor man,
Beggar man, thief,
A doctor,
A lawyer,
A minister,
A priest.'

While somewhere in the yard a group sang, 'A big ship sailing through the alley, alley-o,' another could chant, 'Hally-galee-galloh,' without putting one another off. A girl who had a bouncing ball (for there were stuffed balls that didn't bounce), was a most popular person. She could often be induced to share her ball with a whole group of girls, enabling them to play one of their many games.

'One, two, three, alearie,
Four, five, six, alearie,
Seven, eight, nine, alearie,
Ten alearie, E, I, O.'

was a one-girl ball-game, in which she bounced the ball on the ground using her hand as a bat and throwing her leg over it at every 'alearie.' Similarly she played:

'Number one, eat your bun,
Throw your leg over,
Throw your leg over,
Naughty boy will never get over,
Throw your leg over, (etc.)'

'Number two, touch your shoe,
Throw your leg over, (etc.)'

'Number three, bend your knee,
Throw your leg over, (etc.)'

bouncing the ball all the time, and throwing her leg over as instructed, up to the number twelve.

A wall-ball game was 'Catch, clap.' In this game a number of girls could play, but only one played at the time, while the others watched. The ball was thrown against a convenient wall, and the player would carry out the instruction in each line of the rhyme before the bouncing ball came back to her hand from the wall.

'Catch, (straightforward)
Clap, (clap hands once)
Roll, (roll arms round one another)
Fold, (fold arms before catching)
Hippersy, (touch hip)
Heel, (touch heel)
Toe, (touch toe)
Ground, (touch ground)
Birl round, (spin once before catching)
Baskey, (catching ball in a basket of intertwined
    fingers reversed).

Then to finish neatly,

'Red, white and blue,' (three little forehand taps off
    the wall)
'One, two, three,' (three little backhands.)

This game grew progressively difficult, as the second time round every action was doubled, and it seldom lasted far into the tripling or quadrupling of each action.

A simpler and more popular game with a ball was Donkey Rounders. This game was not played with the round bat as was the ordinary Rounders the Ulsterman took with him to the United States of America, to give that great country its national game. No. All that was needed was the ball, natural cunning and quick reflexes. The thrower stood in the middle while any reasonable number of players stood around waiting to catch the ball. If a player failed in a catch, one letter of the name

DONKEY was awarded, and so on for each catch missed until the 'donkey' of the game came to light.

The fine points of technique required that you throw the ball at one player while actually looking at another, or feign a throw and then send the ball hard in a different direction. It was a fast, nimble game that could be played with a rag ball and, like all the very best games, cost nothing at all.

A real ball, a rag ball, or even a stone, could be used for that primitive ancestor of hurley and hockey - Shinty. Hooked sticks cut from the hedgerows made this a cheap game also, but players became very attached to their own sticks and swore they could not play as good a game with a strange shinty. Opposing teams bore down on one another ferociously, looking as murderous as their tribal ancestors. The motto was, 'If you can't get the ball, get the shin.' Heaven knew, the very name of the game seemed to bear this out. More truthfully, generations of Shinty players became in time first-rate hockey players, with Doagh's Parkview team known Province-wide. It is reputed to be a libel that they retained the old motto!

Boys had marching games, an off-shoot from their school drill. They could be seen often marching behind some self-appointed leader, chanting one of their marching rhythms or tunes:

'Left, Left,
I had a good home an' I
Left,' (over and over again);

or

'Oh, ma, will ye buy me a,
Buy me a, buy me a,
Oh, ma, will ye buy me a,
Buy me a banana?

'Oh, ma, will ye peel the skin,' etc.

or

'Ma, ma, see the kilties,
Ma, ma, see them here,
Ma, ma, see the kilties,
Comin' frae the Crimee War.
Some o' them hes boots an' stockin's,

134

Some o' them hes nane ava,
Some o' them hes . . . (ahem! modesty prevails!)
Comin' frae the Crimee War!

For these last two songs, it was correct to pinch the nose between finger and thumb, in imitation of the bagpipes.

Children had a strict moral code of their own, with rhymes to fit nearly every situation. To name-callers, one replied:

'Sticks and stones may break my bones,
But names will never hurt me,
And when I'm dead an' in my grave
You'll suffer what you callt me!'

No schoolgirl was ever told in so many words that her underwear was visible or that her posture was immodest. Her friends merely shouted, 'I see up Scotland!'

To those who gave a gift and then wanted it back, there was always the ghoulish mysterious threat:

'Give a thing, take a thing,
Find the Bad Man's Gold Ring!'

To children who insisted on hearing a remark repeated, especially if it was none of their business, came the crushing reminder, 'I don't boil my cabbage twice.'

Children who were asked to swear to secrecy on hearing some tit-bit, had to repeat, licking a finger:

'See that wet,
See that dry,
Cross my heart
And hope to die.'

A test of truthfulness could easily be administered. If a child's word was in doubt, his inquisitor was entitled to take his hand, palm upward, and tickle it very gently with a finger, all the while reciting:

'Tickle-y, tickle-y, on the han',
If you are a funny wee man,
If you laugh or if you smile,
You'll never be a lady's child.'

Any hint of a smile meant instant punishment for a liar, or, of course, for a truthful child who was ticklish.

Daddies sometimes played hand or toe games with their children, from the babyish 'This little pig went to market,' to that hiding game where father had a farthing hidden in one hand and a child just might find it, especially if daddy said his little rhyme often enough:

> 'Navy, navy, nik nak,
> Which hand will you tak'?
> The richt or the wrang?
> I'll beguile ye if I can!'

And what child had not been 'caught' by its daddy placing the spoon, warm from his tea-tin, on his child's unwary hand, as he urged it to 'look at that' out of the window?

Hands could be used for a number of excellent games. You and your friend could each make a fist and try to knock the knuckles off one another. This game was, credibly, called Hardi-knuckles. A gentler lively game was 'Pease parritch hot,' in which the two players faced one another, clapping one another's hands, now together, now singly, with hip-slapping between some claps, as all the time the steady chant went on:

> 'Pease parritch hot,
> Pease parritch cold,
> Pease parritch in a pot
> Nine days old.
> Some like it hot,
> Some like it cold,
> Some like it in a pot
> Nine days old.'

A tea leaf floating on a cup of tea could be spooned out and placed on one fist and then thumped hard with the other fist, while the count of 'One, Two, Three ...' went on. When the tea leaf left the original hand and stuck to the second, you knew exactly how many days it would be until you would meet your true love.

Counting similarly the 'cracks' your fingers gave as you pulled them, you would also know exactly how many days it would be until you would meet your true love. And if it so happened that the number of days turned out to be different in the two cases, why, then, it must just mean that you would have more than one true love!

Little fingers were a very important part of a special charm. If you and your friend happened to say the same word at the same time, you immediately linked your wee fingers together without uttering a single word until you both silently wished. When each of you had said the name of a poet, you might safely disengage fingers. Shakespeare and Wordsworth were very much favoured poets, perhaps because they often appeared in the Readers of the day.

Children loved nonsense - not the 'Alice' or the Edward Lear kinds of nonsense, which were too sophisticated for them - but their own nonsense. Some nonsense was made out of perfectly sensible sentences, turned into what our American cousins might call gobbledegook, by the addition of the same syllables to the end of each word. A favourite example was:

'Ifiky Iiky hadiky myiky guniky Iiky wouldiky shootiky thoniky swaniky iniky thoniky milliky damiky!'

A different, and most useful, kind of nonsense was typified by such an example as:

'Mrs. D, Mrs. I, Mrs. F. F. I,
Mrs. C, Mrs. U, Mrs. L. T. Y.'

Real lovely nonsense came into its own with:

'Ladles and Jellyspoons,
I stand upon a speech
To make a platform.
The train didn't arrive, so
I took a cab and walked it.
I come before you, to stand behind you
And tell you something I know nothing about!'

This might well have been a verbal lampoon on almost any politician you care to name. Sheer nonsense for nonsense' sake was:

'I went to the play-house tomorrow,
I took a front seat at the back.
I fell from the pit to the gallery,
And broke a front bone in my back!'

It would be near impossible to list all the games children played when Edward was King. There was such a richness in living despite the equally real poverty. For next-to-no-expenditure, you might be muggyin' with marlies (marbles), shootin' pops (large marbles), stalking about on stilts made of wood or of empty paint tins, making water mills to turn in streams, playing 'Pigg' where you struck a little balanced stick with another to make it fly as far as possible through the air, spinning peeries with your fingers or with a whip, using the same little whip with hayrope reins to make a pair of hackney ponies of your friends, playing Hindmost-of-Three, or Stag, or Hoist Your Sails, or even that game so very popular with all mothers, Kick the Tin!

If you were stuck and couldn't get out to play because of rain or snow - for play out-of-doors was most popular with children, and understandably encouraged by adults - there were 'Snap Cards,' 'Checkaboord,' 'Forfeits,' 'Consequences,' 'I spy with my little eye,' and 'Hunt the Thimble.' And if all else failed, you could take out your sourness by indulging in that sourest of Ulster pastimes, the saying or singing of objectionable stanzas!

A long standing feud between the Church of Ireland Episcopalians (Piskies) and the formerly penalised Presbyterians (Presbys) was satisfactorily carried on in verse:

> 'Pisky, Pisky, say "Amen."
> Down on your knees and up again!'
> 'Presby, Presby, dinna bend,
> But make good use o' man's chief end!'

But what politician, journalist or other expert could make sense of:

> 'Sleeter, Slatter, Holy Water,
> Sprinkle the papishes every one,
> Learn them all a thing or two
> And send them to H--l with their Orange and Blue!'

Mary certainly preferred that other couplet with faint religious overtones that could encompass the surname of any family requiring to be insulted:

> 'And the Lord said unto Moses,
> "All the (Gaults) have got big noses!" '

138

Chapter 10

Towards the end of her third year, Mary realised that with Lennox and Alfred away from home, she was in effect the head of the family. Aunt Laetitia was the head of the household, for nothing was bought or sold without her say-so. Mostly. But when it came to making hard family decisions, Mary's aunt retreated into a shell made up of maidenly modesty, ignorance of the world and its ways, and a small admixture of self-interest.

In the midst of all her copy books, Readers and slates, Mary found a nagging worry creep into her mind as she occasionally caught sight of Freddie, now a big boy of fifteen, long past school leaving age and one of the Master's senior pupils. What could he, or should he, or would he do? With the Master, he was doing the work that such senior boys did, the Mensuration, long and cross tots, Mental arithmetic, English and Penmanship. At all of these he excelled, but when it came to the other subjects of the curriculum he was just a good average boy, with an amazing dislike of History, amazing to Mary, that is, as she had a genuine devotion to the subject. She wished for one of the old family conclaves, such as all five children had been accustomed to having together in bygone days.

Putting the vain regret behind her, she realised that this was up to her. Frederick could sit quite happily at school all his life, but having received three years' extra tuition, Mary felt it was time he started learning whilst earning. He was ever a good natured boy and pleasantly agreed with her - then left her to it. Aunt Laetitia, when consulted, could contribute nothing of a positive nature by way of suggestions, but negatived any manual work as being 'unsuitable.' Mary became thoroughly exasperated at all the non-help she received, and waited until Lennox's next week end at home. Together this brother and sister who were so close to one another discussed the problem of an amiable, well intentioned and lovable brother who was a good worker and would do absolutely anything to oblige, except go looking for something himself. Together, Mary and Lennox discussed the pros and cons of their problem, strolling through the spring meadow grass by the river, where skylarks soared from almost under their feet to a cloudless pale blue heaven of song. Back and forth, and forth and back, they wandered by the edge of the water, thinking aloud and provoking one another to creative thought.

'Let's think what he can't do,' said Lennox, 'and that way we'll see what's left. He's no good at my job and he never was cut out to be a farmer. Aunt Laetitia would die the death if he went into the mill. His friends would probably all cut him anyway. And he can't labour to any farmer round about. That would be just as bad. In Aunt's eyes, I mean!'

'Oh, fiddlesticks!' said Mary. 'I get so fed up with her notions - and *their* notions too, if it comes to that. Why shouldn't anybody work in the mill if they want to?'

'Well, he doesn't want to,' said Lennox, 'so that's that. Now, what is he good at?'

'Eating,' said Mary, who always got uncharitable when worried.

Lennie laughed.

'Chocolates!' he said, and they both burst out laughing until their sides ached, and they almost reeled into the river in the near-hysteria of the relieving laughter.

During the previous winter, Fred, who was a chivalrous boy, had accompanied a lady visitor home to Doagh village on a dark, cold night. Mary, Aunt Laetitia and Little Sister stayed on a few minutes longer to enjoy the conversation of another guest, the ubiquitous Stanley, who had brought, not his motor cycle this time, but a charming box of chocolates sporting red ribbons and red roses. Mary had cast an eye on it once or twice as it lay on the hall table, while she passed to and fro with the supper tray. No, she decided firmly. She would wait until supper was well on the way to digestion and then they'd share them before Aunt Laetitia retired. As she stood there looking at the box, she heard a little whisper from the dark regions above. Lifting the oil lamp that burnt steadily on the hall table, she tip-toed upstairs and into the baby's room. Moxie was now four and no longer a real baby, but so tiny that everyone thought of her tenderly still. She lay, now quiet, her darkly shadowed eyes gazing at the moving shadows thrown on her ceiling by the lady with the lamp. Just how far Mary was at that time from being a lady may shortly be seen. Moxie smiled at her, turned her back on Mary and the bright light, and promptly fell asleep. Mary tucked her in and went down again.

As she entered the dining room, still used as the family parlour, Little Sister was giggling and talking at once. Since she had entered her teens she was allowed up later.

'And he says, he's afraid of nothing. Nothing on this earth,' she gasped. 'He's afraid of his own shadow, I'll bet. Go on, Stanley. Do it for a joke. Please! *Please!*'

Mary knew at once they were talking of Fred, who was a boastful boy now, priding himself on his courage. Bravery was particularly fashionable at that moment as there was A Man on the Roads. Every country district had A Man on the Roads every winter. Nine times out of ten, he was an invention to add spice and thrills to a winter evening.

Sometimes he arose out of silly pranks played by very young adults or very old children. Alfred had been A Man on the Roads in his time, naturally, complete with one of the best linen sheets that were saved for the Visitors' Room. Fred swore he feared nothing and no one and certainly no Man on the Road. Now, Little Sister had put the idea into Stanley's head that it might be interesting to find out if this were so. Mary, suddenly reverting to the childish side of her nature, threw the lady-like side overboard and joined promptly in the plot. Finally, it was agreed that Mary and Stanley would proceed towards the village until they should meet the returning Fred, and do whatever occurred to them on the spur of the moment.

They padded stealthily round Crawfordstown Turn and along by the new Parish Hall. One on either side of the dark road, they slipped on noiseless feet towards the Mill Dam corner. At the corner itself, they heard the brave boy's boots ringing merrily on the frosty road. The brave boy was helping himself along with a very tuneful whistling of a jazzed up 'Clementine.'

'Aa-aah!' came a low blood-curdling moan from beside the mill leat.

'Aa-aah!' came a high banshee wail from the opposite hedge. Fred took to his heels and raced madly for at least a hundred paces. At that point he bent down swiftly and gathered up a handful of rough stones from the road surface. The ghosts made some little noise as they drew nearer to him.

Ping! One stone flew too near to Mary for comfort.

'*I* see you,' cried Fred. '*I* know who you are. Don't you come any nearer me,' and ping! went another stone in Stanley's direction. It could not have been more obvious that Fred

141

certainly did *not* know who 'they' were.

Every now and then a stone hurtled in the direction of the conspirators, who became more discreet than valorous in their following. They stood silent at last, listening. No more stones came their way. For a few further seconds they waited, their breathing fast, their hearts pounding, for they had almost succeeded in frightening themselves. Then, on silent tiptoes, they raced together to Bridge House where an excited Little Sister waited by the hall door.

'Such nonsense,' said Aunt Laetitia, as she carried her lighted candle past the newly arrived conspirators, and made her way with ramrod back up the stairs. 'And it's quite time you were home, Stanley.'

'Oh, yes of course, certainly, yes,' said Stanley. 'Good night, ma'am.'

'Good night,' said Aunt Laetitia and swept round the first landing out of sight. Her bedroom door shut with what in anyone else would have been a bang. Mary nipped Stanley's arm.

'Where is he?' she whispered.

'Yes, where is he? Where is he?' said Little Sister.

'What do you mean, "Where is he?"? He's gone. That is, he's somewhere. How do I know where he is?' Suddenly sobered, the three tiptoed silently into the dining room and noiselessly closed the door. Gently, Mary took the tongs and made up the dying fire. All three wore a chastened air.

'I'd better wait a wee while,' said Stanley cautiously.

'Yes, you certainly had,' said Mary. It suddenly seemed all Stanley's fault.

'Oh, where *is* Freddie?' said Little Sister. 'Do you think he is still hiding down in a hedge afraid to come home?'

Mary had visions of the mill leat with its perilous water and the dark dam.

'Not at all,' she said sharply. 'He'll be here soon, you'll see. In five minutes, I'll put on the kettle. That'll bring him.'

But in twenty-five minutes there was still no Freddie. By now worried out of their wits, the three slipped out together into the dark night. All round the garden, all along the hedgerows, all the way back to where the 'ghosts' had started their wailing, they tiptoed, calling softly, identifying themselves and sounding like Victorian melodramatic performers as they implored their long-lost brother to come home. All the way back they came.

The supper tray stood untouched on the dining room sideboard.

'There's something wrong if he's not here for his supper,'

said Little Sister, who had no illusions about her skinny but nearest and dearest brother.

'Oh, I know, I know. Stop talking,' said Mary unfairly.

'You'd better get home, Stanley. We needn't have two lost boys!' With slight demur, Stanley went.

'I'll call early in the morning to make sure he's safe,' he said and went off soberly into the night. The hall door closed noiselessly behind him. Mary picked up the unused supper tray.

'Bring the lamp,' she said to Little Sister. The two girls went out of the dining room and along the passage way to the kitchen, the younger in front holding the oil lamp aloft.

'Hi! wait a minute,' said Mary, with ungenteel suddenness. As the lamp had shone on the polished hall table, something was missing. They had all forgotten about Stanley's chocolates in the fuss. They were no longer there. Mary's heart gave a bound. She dumped the tray on the hall floor, grabbed the lamp from Little Sister and hared up the stairs as fast as the flaring flame would allow.

There, angelic on its pillow, was Fred's curly head, eyes closed, genuinely asleep, mumbling only a little incoherently and turning, like baby Moxie, from the light. Round the boyish lips was the stain of Bournville, and there, on the floor, the remains of the brave boy's reward for courage (and stealth) - a messed-up, completely empty chocolate box, with little crinkled brown cups lying negligently among red ribbons and roses.

When Mary and Lennox had recovered sufficiently from their old giggles brought on by the memory of chocolates, they continued by the plashy water and the drooping willows to talk, not of Fred's past, but of his possible future.

'Now he *is* good at writing and counting,' said Mary, 'and I think we're going to have to shove him in that direction. I mean, using the bits of talent he's got. Of course,' she added, 'he does sing beautifully, but I don't see anyone making a living at that.'

'Me neither,' said Lennox inelegantly, plucking a branch of meadow-sweet to use as a fly swat. 'I sing beautifully too, but where does it get me?' And impromptu he dropped into an impassioned delivery of 'The Rosary,' addressed to the meadow-sweet:

> 'The hours I spent with thee, dear heart,
> Are as a string of pearls to me.
> I count them over every one apart,
> My Rosary! My Rosary!'

It was true they could all sing, thought Mary. Except herself. And even though they were unlikely to make fortunes by their voices, she still envied them and thought them so fortunate in having this heavenly gift of song.

'I'll tell you one thing it does for you,' said Mary. 'It brings you marvellous friends like Billy Corr and Willie Connor and the rest. They paint. You sing.'

'And you admire. That's the most necessary thing of all,' said Lennox kindly, for he knew Mary so much wanted to sing or paint or have a gift for something. 'We couldn't do without you. What's a singer without an audience? An admiring audience, too,' and he unthinkingly tickled his sister's nose with the meadowsweet.

At once Mary burst into sneezes and Lennox into floods of contrition. 'It's all right,' said Mary. 'Dever bind,' and she sneezed and wept cheerfully.

'Why don't you see if they'll take him in the office of one of the mills?' said Lennox, stopping in his tracks as one on whom a dawn breaks. 'Now, there's something he could do. And do well.'

'Barvellous,' said Mary. 'Dow, why didn't I think of subthing like that? Come od, quick. We'll put it to hib and bake him say he will, and then he can't back out.'

'He won't back out,' said Lennie. 'Once he's pushed in he'll be happy enough. You'll see.'

'Well, you got pushed id and you're dot very happy,' said Mary, regarding her favourite with streaming eyes of affection. 'Why don't you look for a different place? Still gardening, but dot with That Man!'

'I'll finish my time,' said Lennox. 'Anyhow, I don't pay much attention to what he says. Old goat. When I'm qualified, I'll move on. I'd like to see something of the world. And there's always Craigavad to look forward to. And Herrons! And Home!'

Although Mary agreed with him pleasantly enough as they moved towards the meadow gate into the yard, she had one dreadful sinking moment as he tossed off casually, 'see something of the world.' Was his own world not big enough?

It seemed to Mary that she had just grown fond of someone when they were taken from her. She never knew how much she loved them till they were gone and she couldn't let them know how she felt. Mother. And Pappy. And Alfred. But not Lennie. Never Lennie. As they moved towards the back door, she determined fiercely that nobody would ever take Len away from her. Never.

Fred was seated already at the Sunday tea table, waiting patiently for the rest of the family to come from wherever they were and join him. As he waited he absentmindedly ate dry bread from the Belleek plate. Setting the tea table was his contribution to the Sunday chores.

Little Sister and Moxie were absorbed in making daisy chains on the front lawn that never used to allow a daisy to grow. Mary and Lennox came through from the kitchen with fresh salad and a tea pot.

'Where's Aunt Tishy?' asked Lennox, reverting to his childish name for her that his aunt so disliked.

'Bed,' said Fred succinctly, 'and she's doing the Litany after tea, so be warned. Pass the salad.'

Mary knocked on the dining room window. Little Sister peered short-sightedly in her direction and waved. She dragged Moxie up by the hand and they both ran to the front door, up the steps and through to the dining room.

'Hands,' said Mary tersely, and obediently Little Sister hauled Moxie off again to the pantry sink to have her hands wiped clean. Her own didn't need attention, she reckoned, looking at them admiringly. They were small and very dainty. She decided that when she was grown up and rich, she would wear beautiful rings, diamonds probably. They would be becoming. Together, she and Moxie went back to the others and Sunday tea.

Robert Andrew, 'Clerk Rab,' was, though very young, the most important man in the Doagh Flax Spinning Company. Apart, that is to say, from the members of the Wilson family who owned and ran their own mill. Mary, having made up her mind to 'shove' Frederick, acquainted him of that fact after tea, and the very next day walked straight to the mill from school without calling in at home on the way, lest her resolution falter. Fred had been most amiable and agreed that he would like such a job and agreed further that he wouldn't like to go and ask for it. He cleared the tea table in token of his gratitude, although that was strictly Mary's chore.

After tea, while the westering sun still shone in at the dining room bay, the family prepared to go upstairs for Aunt Laetitia's Litany. Once every few weeks she would deliberately take a whole day in bed, now that she was in her sixties. She would take a Saturday or Sunday when there was someone to take charge. But even though she couldn't lie in bed of a Sunday *and* go to Church, she managed a very good compromise by instituting the reciting of the Litany. She played the minister

145

while the kneeling family played the congregation. Moxie was the one who really appreciated the religious exercise since, on her occasional visits to her Stevenson aunts in Donegal, she was part of *several* daily services of Family Prayers that took up a lengthy period before every meal, just when a very little girl would be dying of hunger. Like Aunt Frances Stevenson, Aunt Laetitia read the Lesson for the Day, but she reserved this for Sundays only. Having got rid of the Lesson, as it were, she settled down to do herself good at her latter end.

'... have mercy upon us miserable sinners,' intoned Aunt Laetitia. The family suitably asked for mercy in similar response, but felt little sin and less misery. Over and over again, they had heard the beautiful words that were only to grow in meaning as life progressed. In the flower of youth they were doing a favour to (or suffering a punishment from) their aunt. Aunt Laetitia, upright in her white bed, night-gowned and night-capped, a white shawl about her shoulders, showed risen blue veins in her fine, tremulous hands as she turned the gilt-edged pages.

'O holy, blessed and glorious Trinity, three Persons and one God, have mercy upon us miserable sinners.'

To this strophe, came the children's antistrophe.

'O holy, blessed and glorious Trinity, three Persons and one God, have mercy upon us miserable sinners.'

Mary shifted her knees which were knobbly and insufficiently protected from the bedroom floor. She had forgotten her usual precaution of getting a corner of the bedside rug. She put down a hand and arranged a double fold of her skirt under her knees and buried her head in her hands on the chair seat again.

And they called upon their God to deliver them from all sorts of things, likely and unlikely. From evil, mischief, sin, the craft and assaults of the devil; from God's wrath, everlasting damnation, blindness of heart, pride, vain-glory, hypocrisy, envy, hatred, the deceits of the world, the flesh and the devil; from lightning, tempest, plague, pestilence, famine, battle, murder, and sudden death; from all sedition, privy conspiracy, rebellion; from false doctrine, heresy, schism, hardness of heart, and contempt of God's Word.

'Good Lord, deliver us,' said the family.

Mary found her mind wandering, as it wickedly did when she didn't force herself to concentrate. What *was* schism?

She came to as Aunt Laetitia became more sombre.

'In all time of our tribulation; in all time of our wealth; in the hour of death, and in the day of judgment.'

'Good Lord, deliver us,' said everybody happily.

Mary noted in passing that there was a definite balance in all the petitions. Could it be possible that 'tribulation' was opposed to 'wealth?' It wouldn't surprise her.

She came back to Aunt Laetitia's request to God, not only for their own gentle, elderly Rector, but that it might please God to illuminate all Bishops, Priests and Deacons.

'Hear! Hear!' thought Mary, which was as good an Amen as any.

The rest besought God to hear them. Moxie was definitely getting restless, Mary noticed, peeping through between each pair of fingers, one after the other.

'That it may please Thee to further the work of the Church, and to send forth labourers ...'

Mary heard no more. 'Labourers!' She must, she just *must*, obtain an opening for Fred tomorrow. He was a nice, good boy, well-mannered and good-natured. He was dependable if unimaginative, polite, popular, industrious.

'That it may please Thee,' Aunt Laetitia went on remorselessly, 'to defend and provide for the fatherless children ...'

'Oh, yes, please,' said Mary intensely to the prickly horsehair seat. '*Please!*'

Her head fell further into her hands in the strength of her emotion.

'Son of God, we beseech Thee to hear us.'

'O Christ hear us.'

'O Christ hear us.'

'O Lord,' said Aunt Laetitia, 'deal not with us after our sins.'

'No, no,' agreed Mary thinking of her giddiness and love of dancing. (It couldn't be a sin, could it?)

'Neither reward us according to our iniquities,' she said firmly with the others, taking no chances.

At last the blessed words fell from Aunt Laetitia's lips, the entreaty that the grace of Jesus, the love of God, the fellowship of the Holy Ghost might be with them evermore.

Mary suddenly felt at peace. She felt, too, the strength rise in her. Tomorrow she would see Clerk Rab . . .

And here she was now, waiting outside the Doagh Mill office, some of her certainty fled, her hands shifting her books about nervously. The door opened. Young Mr Andrew smiled. 'Come in,' he said, and stood aside to let her pass.

Fred got his job.

Chapter 11

On the third day of July in the year of our Lord nineteen hundred and seven, Mary became nineteen years of age, reached her full height of five feet two inches and prepared to start her fourth year as a Monitress. She had become a reasonably accomplished Infant Teacher with a real predilection for this work. She was still No Needlewoman, but kept trying until her naturally stiff fingers became even stiffer with tension. She just *had* to pass that needlework examination at the end of her five years.

She could not really understand, in any of her few candid moments of self-examination, just why she was as stiff as a dick-pot when it came to fine sewing, and as nimble as a mountain goat when it came to dancing. She had also some of the other giddy characteristics of this lively animal.

Dancing was not an amusement of which Aunt Laetitia could fully approve. She could approve of Aunt Fletcher's now-grown-up family going to balls in Dublin or London, but for her country bred nieces and nephews at the Bridge House, she could find no suitable partners nor suitable settings. Mary muttered under her breath and, sad to relate, skipped nimbly out of her bedroom window to join Lennie and Fred, and Fred's Winifred and Stanley Wilson for a Grand Ball in Ballyclare Market House. Aunt Laetitia, Little Sister and Baby Moxie slept the sleep of the untroubled innocent.

The guilty Mary was equally untroubled as the light-hearted party of young folk walked in the late Autumn night to Ballyclare, their pumps under their arms, white gloves kept clean in their pockets until they should actually take the floor. Even Aunt Laetitia would have had to admit that theirs was an utterly respectable group. Or perhaps, on second thoughts, she wouldn't. In her young day, all such youthful parties would have had at least one elderly chaperone. Eventually, she did come to a kind of compromise with modern youth over such outings, but never really gave them outright approval.

The Farmers' Ball was only one of the many dances during the Ballyclare Season. These ranged from Surprise Parties in some defenceless soul's house where a bit of a hooley took place, through Barn Dances in some more willing soul's out-house, to the full fig Balls in the Assembly Room above the Market House. Mary enjoyed social life hugely and was prepared to dance till morning, but Lennie on his outings with his family during his visits home, insisted on reasonable hours and, sur-prisingly perhaps, was obeyed.

The ballroom was decorated by a mysterious body called The Committee who seemed to delight in electing themselves year after year, and in putting a great deal of voluntary work into creating a successful evening. Guests arrived on foot, in traps, side cars and gigs. A few came by cab, driven to and from the Ball in the grand manner by one of the Ballyclare jarvies. The mellow light of oil lamps shed a warm glow on bunting and garlands in the gay ballroom, which served as Concert Hall and Lecture Theatre as well. Alas, it also served to remind Mary of her infelicitous appearance as a non-combatant in the pianistic world with the ghastly 'Band on the Pier.' This humiliation was immediately thrust from her mind along with the thought of her fellow duettist, the Master's brother. For he in turn called up a vision of the Master, who would have been quite certain that Mary was dancing along the primrose path. (But she had always liked primroses.)

The gentlemen were dressed as formally as their pockets and wardrobes would allow. A young man in his 'best' suit was admissible, but more and more of the decent country folk aimed at black ties at least, and, as time went on, even white ties became more and more *de rigueur*. The young ladies knew very well that they were there not merely to dance but to put their feminine charms in the shop window. Hours were spent on their toilettes beforehand.

One pretty girl Mary long remembered may serve as exemplar for all. Her name was Lily, and it was just possible that this fact induced her to do a delicate imitation of the lovely Mrs Langtry. Her ball-gown was of pink silk with a moulded cross-over bodice displaying white arms and decolletage. The fullness of the skirt was drawn to the back, so that a smooth, unbroken line fell from waist to toetip in front, and a sprung skirt at the back fell in gleaming folds to a tiny train. Her dark hair was fashionably puffed all round, while two cunning tendrils fell from the velvet

149

camellias pinned beside her back comb. Her fashionable elbow length gloves, her foam of lacy frills at her bosom and her choker of many 'pearls' completed an ensemble that was as charming as it was banal.

Mary had one solitary dress of serviceable blue, which fact troubled her not at all. She came for the fun and the dancing. Her sole ambitions were to dance every dance, eat a good supper and escape the notice of both Aunt Laetitia and the Master. She did, however, have a secret addition to her wardrobe which by misfortune did not remain a secret for ever. Little Sister was now a rather large fifteen, an excellent pianist and a quite brilliant singer with already the Gold Medal of the Ard-Feis Ceol to her credit. As a consequence, Aunt Laetitia had had a beautiful dress made for her of pale silk lustre. This was intended for the Concert platforms of Belfast, Derry and Dublin. Mary found that it was also quite serviceable for Dances. The only thing that lessened her stolen pleasure was the fact that Little Sister was still little about the feet, so that it was by no means unknown for our Cinderella to appear at the nearest thing to the Prince's Ball in crystal-embroidered pearly silk with Size Six brogues just peeping underneath.

The youthful party ascended the well-worn wooden stairs from the level of the Market House to the ballroom above. The girls left their coats - Mary still in her Donegal tweed - and dusty walking shoes in the office of the main hall. They tidied themselves before the small temporary mirror hung in the office to convert it into a Ladies' Cloak Room. A further convenience was supplied by a zinc bucket behind a temporary curtain, sagging slightly across a corner of the little room. All those with friends living in the town cultivated their acquaintance carefully just before any Dance, so that they would have a more acceptable amenity to which to withdraw.

Already the band of two fiddles and one piano was singing out a Viennese Waltz. Mary was itching to be on the floor and she hurried the other four to a group of empty chairs amongst those ranged round the walls. Just as they claimed these and all put on their white gloves, the dance ended, and the politely applauding dancers returned to their seats, each lady escorted thereunto by her stiffly bowing partner. Mary sneezed.

She always sneezed at Dances. Her paternal inheritance of asthma and hay fever reared its ugly little head in reaction to the pounds of French chalk on the dusty wooden floor. She cared not a fig for this, but, like her generation, thrust such small ailments firmly down again out of sight. Nothing should spoil her enjoyment of the dance. As the night wore on, the French chalk would rub the old floor to a gloss under the dancers' feet.

The band, in white ties and tails, shuffled sheet music behind their two palms and three flower pots on the platform. The Master of Ceremonies stepped up beside them. In full carrying voice he announced, 'Ladies and Gentlemen, pray take your partners for the Quadrilles.' All of the dancers had little printed Programmes which were no more than a folded card with deckle edges and a silk twist in the fold to carry the tiny pencil. Mary glanced at hers, still empty except for the Order of dances, but not to remain so for long. She pounced on Lennox. What else are brothers for at a dance than to fill in when there's no-one else? Good-humouredly, he put W.L.S.D. at the Quadrilles, the second dance on Mary's card. Thank goodness, she had missed no more than one. He noted it in his own programme and led his sister to the long lines for the Quadrilles formed down the whole length of the room. Stanley kindly volunteered to guard the chairs, for the room was gradually filling with more and more guests. Frederick, now a skinny, amiable youth of seventeen, led his lady love, Winifred, to join the dance. She was a large, immensely good-humoured girl, some years older than Freddie. He adored her all his life, married her eventually and they truly lived happily ever after.

Stanley watched the dancers. The Master of Ceremonies duly performed one of his main tasks, which was Leading Off each dance he announced. All the dancers weaved in and out, long lines meeting and parting, each time turning about to give the gentlemen new partners to lead up the middle and down again. The Master of Ceremonies had a worrying time, but never willingly gave up the job to anyone else. He considered the worst part over when he led off for the first dance of the evening, for which he had to choose as partner the most important lady present. Many a faint-heart played for safety by leading off with his own wife.

By the time the two brothers and sister with Winifred in tow returned to their chairs, several young men were standing with Stanley, more than ready to initial the girls' programmes. Waltzes, Mazurkas, Polkas, Schottisches, Quadrilles and Lancers were claimed in full to Mary's gratification. She knew that on the morrow she would suffer the same racking coughs that sent Aunt Laetitia's head into purdah with Potter's. But, like every nineteen-year-old ever born, the Biblical Text she approved most was, 'Sufficient unto the day is the evil thereof.'

At the end of two hours' non-stop dancing, even Mary was

'The band, in white ties and tails, shuffled sheet music behind
their two palms and three flower-pots on the platform. The
Master of Ceremonies stepped up beside them.'

glad to hear the Master announce the first supper. The five youngsters had trysted together for supper rather than go down with other partners, so that when their Cicerone called for twenty couples he got nineteen-and-a-half. Chattering in the throng of thirty-nine dancers trooping down the back staircase to the Market House below, Mary stole a mischievous glance at Fred. His face wore the look of glad and innocent expectation it had worn ever since she could remember when he contemplated food. Yet he never got any fatter. Just longer.

The Supper Room, by day the Market House where stiff carts were weighed and produce bought and sold, did not disappoint him. The Committee always took immense trouble with their suppers. These seemed to offer an outlet to some creative urge, and the planning, preparation and serving were carried out with happy thoroughness. A very long table, to seat forty, ran the full length of the supper room. The boards and trestles were concealed under snowy linen damask cloths. All the Committee members had brought their finest china, best silver, crystal and cutlery. Buffet suppers were never served anywhere in Mary's youth. Everyone was seated and sated. Moulds of tinted jellies of pink and green and yellow wobbled at intervals the whole length of the huge table. They were flanked by sherry trifles in crystal bowls, attended in turn by silver dishes of whipped cream. Boudoir fingers in glasses like pretty little celery sticks helped Frederick to stow away something solid with such kickshaws as trifles and jellies. More boudoir fingers held up Charlottes Rousses that would have been quite a credit to Mrs Beeton, judging by the illustrations in that famous work at home in the Bridge House attic. (There was little need for it in the kitchen.) Dainty sandwiches garnished with water cress were mere bouchées to tempt the appetite to off-set them with delicate petits-fours. Evening gowned hostesses hovered round with their best silver tea pots. Mary sighed happily and stoked up energy for the second half of the evening.

No alcohol was served at supper. No rowdyism was ever heard of at a Dance. The Country Ball was probably at its peak of formal informality, prosperity without vulgarisms, gaiety with good manners. It was also one of the High Water Marks of Ulster snobbery, for in a society that approached classlessness in everyday life, no factory worker would have been welcomed or indeed expected at such Balls. To do the lower manual workers justice, it apparently never entered their heads to go. Mary heard one elderly matriarch declaim as though it were a tenet of religion. 'Let farmers' sons marry on farmers' daughters, and

153

labourers marry on labourers'.' That matriarch was ruler of ten acres and a tumbledown farmhouse. Mary's sense of the ludicrous almost brought her to the disgrace of laughing aloud, but she managed to retain her self-control, and play lip service to a creed in which she had little belief. Her self-control really had improved with the years.

Whirling unthinkingly in the gaiety of the dance, Mary had no thought for the morrow. While there were partners she would dance. Just fleetingly she hoped for one second that Aunt Laetitia would not be visited by an uncharacteristic concern, and look to see if Mary were sleeping well. It was so unlikely that she put such a thought where it should be, under her feet and danced on it. The small morning hours came. Lennie took out Pappy's hunter and looked at it. 'Nuisance,' thought Mary, 'He's thinking of going.' He was.

Surprise parties were no surprise to the guests; only to the hosts. A group of young people would gather and decide secretly to have a party in someone's house. Everyone would be told what to bring along for the supper - some sandwiches, a cake, some buns or scones. The hosts did nothing but provide the meeting place, and many were the looks of amazement on the faces of decent people when they were met at their own back door by a crowd of youngsters shouting, 'Surprise! Surprise!' There is no record of anyone's ever having objected to a surprise party being held in his house. This may have been simple good nature. It just may, on the other hand, have been wise policy. Young folks then got up to lots of tricks, from neatly closing up the chimney of your home with fresh-cut sods so that you were smoked out, to the mildest jape of all, carrying off the gate of your yard or garden. Some jests were so wild that one might have been driven to think that not only the garden gates were unhinged.

A Barn Dance was something else again. The youths and girls attending it were rather older than the surprise party goers. There was much objectionable truth in the old lady's statement when she said that farmers' sons should marry only farmers' daughters. There were not so very many meeting places for them, so barn dances provided one opportunity for winter meetings of the young of both sexes, just as the Picnic did in summer. In passing, the Picnic deserves a mention, if it were only to say that it was not an outing that had the slightest connection with food! It was a summer's evening gathering together of local boys and girls in a new mown and cleared hay field. Here, they played games till twilight fell, when those girls who had been eyed out were escorted to their homes.

Many a time romance began similarly at a Barn Dance. Mr and Mrs William John Ferguson met at a Barn Dance. It was held at her home, and as one of the hostesses she was carrying plates of cakes, offering them to the guests. When Kate offered one to William John, he looked at the little heart-shaped tarts for a moment and then said, 'I'll have one if I can have yours along with it.' This was a storybook tale, for they did marry and live happily ever after, or very, very nearly so.

For a Barn Dance, all the straw in the barn was pushed and piled at one end. Barn Dances took place at the back end of the year, after New Year, but before spring brought days and days of unending work to every farmer and his family. The winter supply of food for beasts had decreased sufficiently to leave a lot of room in the barn. This was always a second floor storeroom entered by an outside staircase of stone or wood. The great storeroom ran the full length and breadth of all the byres and stables below. When the straw had been put aside, the ceiling, walls and floor were swept thoroughly. Some people even white-washed the walls. The place was decorated with much-used bunting and hung with hurricane lamps (oil) or storm lanterns (candles). No farmers' children needed to be told to be careful about flame in the so-inflammable place. They had grown up with this greatest of all 'Don'ts.' In all the hundreds of Barn Dances Mary knew, she never once heard of a fire occurring.

Rough seats ran round the walls of the barn. They were of planks and beams of wood set on bricks, the whole covered with vari-coloured quilts to pad them and to add to the colourful scene. Some people went to the lengths of borrowing the local church forms to seat their guests, but this was not as popular as it might have been, since it involved inviting the Cleric or, even worse, some Elders, out of politeness. If they had come, they might not just have been all that welcome. Any spare chairs from the farmhouse were carried up for the older people present, chaperons who were almost *required* to be there. The removal of these chairs from kitchen and parlour left room for lots of the tables to be spread with the kind of supper only a farmer's wife could set up.

She would have felt disgraced without at least six kinds of sandwiches and as many sorts of fancy breads and scones. These formed the main padding of the meal which was then over-laid with cream cakes, brandy snaps, currant squares, sponge cakes, Victoria sandwiches, Genoese pastries, Empire biscuits, Battenberg cake, coconut buns, jam tarts and custard tarts, apple pie, shortbread, trifles and jellies. Cream from the milk crocks was plentiful, as was the fresh butter for scones or gleaming jam for the fancybreads. The guests would come down in batches of perhaps twenty at a time, and even when the last group had gone up again to the barn, there was enough for them to start all over again if they wished.

No Barn Dance was complete without the fiddler. He was treated better than any guest there, for he was unpaid. (He did, however, accept a hefty tip!) Being unpaid, he could throw a temperament if he wished, and he let everyone understand this clearly. Therefore, he was fed like a fighting-cock and, unlike the others present, was given a drop of 'the crather' to sweeten him. By the time he had really got going in a Schottishe or the Lancers, he no longer cared so much about the niceties of etiquette, being carried away like the dancers in the jovial swing of the music. How the floor bounced and spurted dust under their feet! How the cotton, gingham and linen dresses of the girls swayed and swung in the uproarious Lancers! Laughter resounded even above the shrill fiddle, when a lowing of cows or neighing of horses came from below, as cattle reminded men that they had work to do tomorrow.

No Barn Dance went on to a late hour. Instead, it started as soon as possible after lowsing time, and came to an end a little after ten o'clock. Everyone had an early start next morning. Only at such grand functions as a Farmers' Ball or a Hunt Ball was the son or daughter of the house allowed out till three in the morning, with the luxury of 'a long lie and a tay breakfast' to follow. The barn dancers never met the Knocker-Upper going round villages rousing mill workers for their day's toil, as some of the patrons of a Ball were reputed to have done. More than that, it was said of at least one young man going home from a Ball at which he had been a Committee Member, that he complained of having done *two* days' work when he met on the road children who were only 'half-timers.' A cruel little class joke, and not at all the sort of which Mary could approve. Like her aunt before her, she had ways of letting people know how she felt. She felt for 'half-timers' a great compassion and a real affection, and was instantly enraged if anyone slighted them.

Chapter 12

October, nineteen hundred and seven, brought the usual Hallowe'en holidays. These were not given to celebrate either the Eve or the Feast of All Souls, but for what the English called 'potato picking' and Mary's pupils 'pritta gatherin'.' It well behoved every Master of a country school to arrange such a vacation. If he had not done so, the pupils would have stayed away anyhow. The last of the Harvest, the potato crop, must be got in, even under the shadow of the dreaded 'Board' man.

The Harvest Thanksgiving Services had already taken place in the Parish Church. Mary's official thanksgiving there always took place on the last Sunday in September. The congregation singing 'All is safely gathered in,' when it so obviously wasn't, worried Mary not a whit. She speculated that if God lived in Eternity, a small matter like dates in Time wasn't liable to perplex Him. She reckoned that such singing could do naught but emphasise the great virtue of Faith. Not so, one of her Rectors. With a degree of pedantry, though with equal dependence on the bountiful Giver of All, he insisted that the congregation sing, 'All *will* be safely gathered in.' This caused no small confusion, and there were always those who hadn't caught up with the other worshippers by the end of the verse.

But it was, apparently, essential that the Service be held on this Sunday to give everyone a fair crack of the whip at Harvest Thanksgivings, for, from the anciently established Methodist Church in Doagh kicking off the Thanksgiving season on the Third Sunday in September to the very last Presbyterian Service in October, Sunday after Sunday of Thanksgivings took place round all the Churches, with the less stable members of the Christian faith pursuing them from church to church. Undoubtedly, this had some ecumenical worth, but while the congregations gallivanted from church to church, the loyal unfortunates whose turn it wasn't had a thin time of it.

Mary loved her Harvest Service. The beautiful Parish Church was fragrant with sharply odoriferous chrysanthemums, brilliant with dahlias, plenteous with oats and barley, down to earth with parsley, leeks, turnips, great cabbages, and every delicious vegetable that filled garden and field, and mouth watering with polished apples. Atop a shelf-like projection on a prominent pillar was a little scarlet row of the new love-apples, for which all had not as yet acquired a taste, one school of thought eating them with sugar, the opposing school favouring salt.

During these 'pritta gatherin'' holidays, Mary and Little Sister went blackberrying. Into their tin cans went the plump juicy fruit - well, mostly into the cans. They invariably returned home bearing some faint resemblance to their Presbyterian friends, popularly called 'Black Mouths.' Baby Moxie trotted after them, a pint tin in her hand, gathering up the low-slung riches hanging their heads in the grassy dykes, but eating none, for of this highly allergic family, she was the most allergic of all. No fruit passed her baby lips, just as an egg was to her anathema.

Home again with their free gifts from the hedgerows, they all watched while Aunt Laetitia boiled the juicy blackberries in a little water until the pot was a seething mass of black fragrant liquid filled with suspended seeds. Mary hung the wooden framed jelly bag from its appointed hook in the pantry, and all day and all night the glorious drip, drip went on. Next morning, Mary used a pint tin to ladle the juice back into its enamel pot with a pound of fine white sugar accompanying each measureful. She mustn't squeeze the jelly bag or touch it in any way or the eventual jelly would be cloudy. Aunt Laetitia supervised the boiling of juice and sugar, and the heating of jam jars in the oven. Plout! Plout! Plout! went the boiling jelly, and after about fifteen minutes it changed its tune and went pianissimo, Crackle! Crickle! Crackle! Then Aunt Laetitia allowed Mary to spoon a little into a china saucer, and set this to cool on the marble slab near the pantry window. The three girls gathered round and watched the saucer, until Mary lifted it and drew one light finger tip across the cooled surface. An ever increasing wrinkle followed the finger. The jelly had jelled. Now, to fill the pots for winter storage. Laboriously Little Sister wrote sticky labels saying 'Bramble Jelly' and stuck them on the sealed jars. Then on to the high pantry shelf they went, cold and dry, beside evocative summer labels that said 'Raspberry,' 'Strawberry,' 'Blackcurrant Jelly,' 'Gooseberry Marmalade' and the omnipresent 'Rhubarb and Ginger.'

158

Not all household chores were as greatly to Mary's liking as pickling and preserving. One job she did first thing in the morning, for no other reason than to get it out of the way. This was the preparation of the lamps, which had to be done every day. It was instilled into all members of the family that when they came down in the mornings, they bring their lamps or candlesticks with them. There the lamps sat together on a back shelf, upstairs lamps and downstairs lamps, jewelled lamps of brass and glass, ruby, sapphire and emerald, now smelly, dimmed and oily. The candles in their holders got only a wipe to keep them dust free, but the lamps had to be cleaned thoroughly.

First, Mary removed all the globes, those fine glass chimneys that kept draughts from the burning wicks. She set them very carefully in a row. Then, turning the brass raising-screw of each lamp in turn, she gently wiped the cotton wicks of round, double or single burners, to remove the deposit of carbon. Then each wick was lowered and trimmed so that no long end of cotton remained to blacken the glass. Wicks trimmed and cleaned, the whole head was then unscrewed, and our wise virgin made sure that every lamp was topped up with pungent paraffin. Lamps cleaned every day, burned with a clear, soft light and almost no smell.

Having reassembled the filled lamps, Mary then cleaned the globes inside and out, breathing on the glass gently, and rubbing it up with tissue paper until those chimneys fairly sparkled. The globes were replaced in their brass holders and the lamps were ready for another night's work. Lamps for the drawing room and dining room had round ground-glass shades. The kitchen had a large hanging lamp in the centre, with a reflector throwing light downwards, as well as a bracket lamp screwed to the wall by the main table. The bedroom lamps were small by comparison, and had carrying handles to their brass or coloured glass bowls.

The colourings of the lamps were not the only factors in Mary's likening them to butterflies. This was one of her flights of fancy when she would birl round and round 'flying' with a precious shining lamp in either hand.

'Butterfly,' she sang. (Well, more or less sang.) 'Butterfly.'

'What on earth are you doing?' said Aunt Laetitia.

'I was just thinking,' said Mary.

'I have heard of some Tom-fool sitting up a pole to think,' said Aunt Laetitia tartly. 'But never dancing with a lamp in each hand. And what, Miss, do you mean "Butterfly"?'

'That's what I was thinking,' said Mary. They have just one

day of looking lovely, and that's the butterfly too. Lovely for a day. You'll see. Tomorrow morning these'll be as oily and stinking as ever.'

'That's not a word ladies use,' said Aunt Laetitia. 'Put those lamps down before something happens to them. Are you or are you not going to Currie's during these holidays? I can't run any day of the week, you know. You'll have to give me time.'

'I have decided, Aunt,' said Mary. 'I'm going by myself.'

'By yourself?' Aunt Laetitia's scanty eyebrows disappeared into her Alexandra fringe. 'Indeed, madam! I suppose you're independent now?'

'It's my money and I want to pick it and order it myself,' Mary was firm.

'Huh!' said Aunt Laetitia, and went into a huff for the rest of the day. But Mary had saved hard and her aunt recognised her right to spend her money her way. After a few hours, that is.

Next day Mary went off to buy her first piece of furniture. She was going to The London House, at Ballyclare's North End, where Mr Currie, the cabinet maker, had his shop, shared by his wife who ran a successful drapery business there too.

Mary chose the design carefully, not too much scroll-work so as to save dusting, good quality mahogany, a long blanket drawer, a full length mirror. Yes, that was just it. How much?

'Two pounds,' said Mr Currie. 'It'll take about a fortnight.'

'Do I pay you now?' said Mary, wanting to get her money handed over safely before anyone else could claim or use it.

'Not at all,' said Mr Currie kindly. 'You see that your wardrobe's just what you want before you pay me a penny. I can always make a few alterations if you want them.

'I see,' said Mary. 'Thank you.' And went home to hide her two pounds.

She hid them even from herself, for she was subject to a strong temptation. She loved sweets. Almost as much as the sweets, she loved the wee sweetie shops which were to be found everywhere. No licences were needed to start up in business and overheads were nil, for the shops were the kitchens of women who could not get out to work in mill or field.

The counter of a wee shop was the kitchen table. After breakfast was over, the family off to work or school, the youngest penned-up or the invalid grannie settled and the dishes washed, the oilcloth covered table was moved so that it almost blocked the doorway to the tiny hall. On it were set the small scales and weights which ranged from a quarter of an ounce to a pound.

160

Few things sold amounted to more than the latter weight, and if anyone wanted two pounds, couldn't it be done at twice? On the wall-shelves where other women kept their good delft tea pot, their rosy cups and their Jubilee mugs, the shop keeper kept a row of glass jars and shiny quart cans of tin, filled with sweeties. More jars sat on the kitchen window sill, a visible temptation to passers-by to come in and spend. There were aniseed balls, black balls, acid drops, bulls' eyes, clove rock and white conversation 'lozengers,' greatly prized by shy young men, with their printed red inscriptions saying, 'Will you marry me?' 'I love you,' or simply 'Sweetheart.' There were wee pink smokers, cachous that perfumed the breath, butternuts, and lucky lumps in any one of which you might find a shiny silver thrupenny-bit. There was liquorice got up as a sweetmeat in many forms - in mouth-size black cylinders, in long ribbons, in laces just like those leather whangs with which men laced their heavy boots, as black pipes with glowing 'tobacco' of red hundreds-and-thousands. There were slabs of toffee at a ha'penny which afforded long flavourful chews. There were dainty oval wooden boxes of sherbet, complete with tiny wooden spoons. These luxurious boxes of sherbet that fizzed deliciously on the tongues and conjured up the exotic East, also cost a ha'penny; but if you didn't have a whole penny or half-penny to spend, you could still get a good paper-poke of dolly mixtures or ju-jubes for a farthing.

Children had need of other things besides sweeties. In their own wee shops they could get marbles, clay pipes for blowing bubbles, dulse, gingerbread men, peeries, whips and pops. Their grannies could get clay pipes too, but in theirs they smoked tobacco. Old women loved their smoke and banked up their little 'baccy fires by covering the bowls with pierced tin covers. Even if the shank of one of these fragile pipes broke, it was still a good smoke as an upside-down cutty, clenched between the lips of an elderly devotee.

Grannies, as well as grandas, loved not just their pipes but their snuff. They had to get their plug or twist at the grocer's, but aromatic snuff could be bought in the wee shop. Snuff wasn't weighed but was measured in a divided tubular tin, one end holding an ounce, the other end half an ounce. A small poke of newspaper was the purchaser's snuff box, a far cry from the gentlemanly elegance of an earlier century. One always knew snuffers by their dust impregnated clothes and blackened nostrils.

Popular with younger women were cloves and cinnamon buds. They chewed these all day long, off-setting the pouce of

161

scutching or the rank smell of tow with the pungent spices. Women depended too on the wee shops for emergency rations. All stocked some baker's bread from Bob on the O.P.B. van - a few loaves, penny baps, tuppeny buns, stomach cakes, butter biscuits, Ballymena biscuits (not biscuits at all, but bread), Paris buns and snowtops.

If a woman ran out of bread, a child was rushed to the wee shop for a loaf. If she had unexpected guests, she could serve a cup of tea, with a hastily procured Paris bun or a snow-top. As well, she could get her paraffin oil or a needed candle. She could buy onions. And if a special event were looming up, she could order real fancy buns, always called 'pastry,' to be left by Bob in time for the Christening, Wake or Wedding. Mary remembered one unfortunate child sitting down on a box of such pastry by accident, and being berated, not just by the owner of the ruined buns, but by Cassie, proprietress of that wee shop. Cassie had a very grand notice in her shop, stuck up where all could see it clearly against its background of garish 'lemonade.' It impressed all who could read it. Those who couldn't soon learnt what it meant. Curlicues and all, it read: 'By not asking for Credit, the unpleasantness of a Refusal will be avoided.'

How Mary loved her wee shops, Cassie's and Grannie Fulton's at the Tinker's Row, and Mary Marshall's in Cogry, and Matilda Cooper's by the Smithy, on the way to the Upper Station and ... but one could go on and on. Mary felt that if ever the wee shops should disappear, they would be sadly, sadly mourned. Not least by herself. In the meantime, she put her two pounds in Pappy's no-longer-used pink porcelain tobacco jar, and closed it up along with Temptation.

Mary's wardrobe was a great source of private pleasure to her as she thought about it during the weeks it was in the making. The pleasure made her excessively good-humoured and she was able to be kind and condescending to all, as an owner of property should be. Thus, when Aunt Laetitia instructed her to call at a Wake-house, she did not demur for once, but agreed so quickly that she couldn't get out of it later. For one of Mary's temperament, nervy, highly strung, given to giggles (that she was fast training herself out of), the silent house of the dead was a sore trial. At Bradshaw's every clock had been stopped at the hour of death. The mirrors were covered in white muslin. For long minutes no one spoke.

Mary wished she had been able still to attend an old-time wake when corpse and crowd seemed joined in a last carouse, and where the maddest practical jokes were played. She did, however, agree with one woman at an old-time wake who, when the fun and games were at their height, declared that it was not really desirable to serve food and drink using the coffin as the table. Mary's friend said her 'heart didn't lie to the meat,' and Mary endorsed her opinion. But anything would have been better than the wake of Andy Bradshaw's wife Minnie.

She had been a tiny woe-begone woman with a small income and a large family. The immense struggle to do her very best for Andy and the 'weans' had been no help in fighting Ireland's dread 'consumption,' and now Minnie was gone, her man and her children left to fend for themselves. Mary knew how that felt, and she determined to be a good neighbour as well as representing her school at the house that provided it with so many pupils. As she sat still on the edge of a chair, having ceremonially viewed the corpse, duly admired it and its coffin and the one pitiful little wreath of artificial flowers in a glass dome, she wished she had brought a bunch of flowers from home. She wished the reign of Nicholson had not finished the good old days of wakes for ever. She wished she was not so much out in the limelight. And she wished above all that somebody would *say* something.

Only the death watch beetle carried on with his busy tick, like a secret, hidden pocket watch. Whispers came from the settle by the fire where sat two buxom wives of small farmers who had obviously called, like her, to pay their respects, and were putting in the time as best they could in sibilant gossip. She wished she was near enough to hear. Their talk would while away her time too. She eyed out a handy chair and waited for it to become vacant. Soon her chance came as the aged aunt who occupied it rose to help in getting tea for all present. Every wake was an endless swarry. This was a blessing for it kept the household busy during the first numb days of bereavement. Mary slipped silently into the vacated seat and prepared happily to eavesdrop.

'Don't gallop in and out,' Aunt Laetitia had said. 'Stay a decent time. Don't wear out your welcome. And there's no need to eat anything. But drink a cup of tea. That will please them. And ...' But Aunt Laetitia's Do's and Don'ts had fallen on stony ground at the last, for Mary was off. Now she was carrying out one of her aunt's commands at least, for she felt, and quite rightly, that her neighbours would help to fill up the 'decent time' that etiquette demanded.

'... so I turned roun an said to him, "Poor Ireland, mony's a fool she has raired." An he niver turnt the word. He knowed better. Upsettin pup. O well, that's the way it is. As ye rair yer pup ye have yer dog. If I toul her onst I toul her a thousan times. But there ye are. An where are ye.'

'True. The truth bites sore. Did ye iver see anythin. like th' way the whole clanjamfry's gatherin in now that niver had a civil word for her an her alive? Hi. Take a wee gleek rount t' yer left. Who's that one? I know the face but I can't put a name on her.'

'Who? O, her. I see who ye mean. That cheeky article. That's our John's wife, a Mawhunnion she wuz till her own name. D'ye min' there wuz one o' them went till America an' done terrible well? Uh, sure ye min' him? A wee tully-eyed buddy that wud nyuck th' cross off an ass? Hi. Is this cake foosty er am I oney imaginin it? What wuz I sayin'? Oh. Ay. Wud nyuck the cross off an ass. An' the ass as weel if ye hadn't yer eye on him. He wuz a right cuddy hesel. D'ye not min' he married a Yank an' when he lands her home who is she but oul Mcanally's dochter an' no a Yank at all. A hard yin thon'll be. She'll niver let her bone go wi' the dog, I bate you any money. O, well, she got a right hallion there for there wuz niver one o'that travalley that wuzn't a ganch. D'you know, she niver lot on she knew a one o' us but juist sut there as mim as ye like. Feth an' she had the hames on him all right - No, dear, no more tea for me, thank you very much all the same. That wuz lovely - that cake *wuz* foosty. I drapped min' b'low the chair. What did you dae wi' yours?'

'Ay. Ay. Ay. I min' her now. A right dafty if iver I seen one. That wuz the one lot on she wud go intae a dwam if she heerd the word "whusky" an' went on wi' a lock o' didoes lik' that. Her! Imagine! An' her oul Da the biggest oul drouth in the Three Kingdoms. When he wuz in the drink he wud mell ye, and when he wuz daft for a naggin he wuz the biggest oul lick-spittle ye cud meet, craikin away about not havin a make an he wud see ye again. Feth he wudn't see me again for he wudn't see me the furst time, not if I seen him furst. There's plenty o' publicans livin' aff the fool's penny wi'out me helping them.'

'A truer word you niver spoke. Hi. It's lucky warm in here. If we get the chanst, we'll slip ower there beside the jamb and get a wee breath from the dure. Oh! ... Pardin'. I hate givin' a rift at a wake for a wake's that deadly. Ye hear iverythin'.'

'Ay. There's not half the stoor at a wake there used tae be. There was a time ye cud have went till a wake an been sure o' a good night's entertainment, but the oul times is all past. No stoor now at all. D'ye think we cud go now like the beggars? - No I s'pose we better wait a minnit or three. That minds me. I sh'udn't a been surprised at Minnie goin' for there wuz Samuel Anra's feyther in the Dathes on Saturday night an oul Mrs Akeson the same week. Always in threes. Isn't that a quare thing when ye think on it? I'm aye terrible glad when I hear the third one for I know then it's no me. Poor Minnie. Oh well, wi' the help o' God an the heat o' the weather it'll rain the morra. Happy is the bride ...'

'An' happy is the corp the rain rains on! One dacent woman wuz Minnie. An' she had a sorry erran' t' th' worl' when all's said an' done. Them unbiddable pups o' youngsters an that gomeril o' a man o' hers. Ugh, well, I s'pose Andy's a dacent enuff buddy in hes way but all I have t' say is, his way's no my way. I wud a stirred his tay wi' the head o' a match long ago. Tell me this and tell me no more, in yer soberiety cud ye bear t' leave we' an eejit like that? Not much o' the lig about him the night, tho'. He's wild sober. Luks as if he dizzent know what en' o' him's up. Well, well! It'll all be the same in a hundert years. But it's lamentable too. I'll·quarely miss Minnie.'

'She wuz the heart o' corn. There wuzn't many like her in a quarter stone. Hi. That's a quare nice shape o' a wee milk joug. That joug over there. Ay. That's the yin. I s'pose they hev got the len o' a lock o' things frae Todds. They niver had much furnishings here an Todds hes lashins. Juist imagin. Sandy Todd'll be sittin' bird-alone in that place when the oul pair goes. I think I'll be at our Jeannie to get a fut in the dure. By my sang, if that lady dizzent get a move on she'll git nobody. The airs of her. She wud make ye boak. Chuck-full o' nonsense. If she's not watchin' she'll git left on the shelf and they'll no even bother tae dust her. There's a rap at the dure. Who's that comin' in? I cannae see from here. Wudn't ye think people wud hev some manners an' a dathe in the house? Who is it? Can ye see? Why-int them ones shift? Stan' up a wee minnit as if ye wur settlin' yer coat better an' ye'll get a gander. That coat's a bit cliver onyway.'

'I will not indeed. I'm that bumfilled I can harry shift. I wish I *cud* shift fur I'm gettin' bristled up at that fire. Speak of angels, that's Todd that's in. *You* better be the yin t'budge and get a crack wi' him. God! Luk at that Andy - dizzent know what en' o' him's up. If you shifted on till that kist, ye wud be

'An' happy is the corp the rain rains on.'

nearly b'side Todd.'

'No. I'll no. I'm not pushin'! It's not in my nature to be pushin'. Nor noan of our ones wuz pushin'. Where's he now? Oh, ay. I see him. I'll juist move a wee bit. But I'm not goin' down hes throat for no man. Nobody'll iver say I'm pushin'! He's not a bad-lukkin' fella that, mind you. Usually if they've money they're like damn-all. That one o' ours is like the swan - she wud die o' pride if it wuzzent fur her feet. But surely t' God wuddent ye think Todd wud soot her? By my sang, I'll give her a hint wi' the toe o' my boot if she dizzent get a move on. Tell me this an' tell me no more ...'

But no more Mary heard, for two mourners exiting neatly at that precise moment, her entertainers moved smartly into their places, which happened by the greatest good fortune to be between 'Todd' and the jamb wall so that the wake was a cause of rejoicing for somebody.

Chapter 13

During the five years of Mary's Monitress-ship, the world of her people changed completely. In the first year, nineteen hundred and three, the great Wyndham Act was passed that gave every Irish farmer his land to own, if he and his dependants paid the annual instalments to the Government over the next sixty-eight years. It made land even more worth fighting for (and land hunger was a deeply passionate emotion with all Irishmen), but more importantly it meant that the bad old age of Landlordism was over for ever.

In Mary's last year, nineteen hundred and eight, David Lloyd George gave to those people of the British Isles too old and infirm to work, the first Old Age Pension of five shillings a week, so that nevermore need anyone suffer the privation and hardship that had been the lot of far too many of the ancient poor in bygone days. Never again would Mary actually see anyone die of starvation, as she had seen not once before, but thrice. The age of the Poor House, too, was over for ever.

These facts, that the Landlords and the Poor Houses had gone, were generalisations only. There were exceptions that would linger on for some years, but the great central fact of life now for English, Scots, Irish and Welsh was the huge red existence on the map of the British Empire. Song, poem and story extolled its virtues, and even in the little mill schools, boys were cock-a-hoop with Jingoism and girls wide eyed with admiration of them. War was somehow in the air. No one could tell quite how or why. Nevertheless everyone from that elderly boy, Edward VII, to the smallest lad (and even lass), appeared constantly in the uniform of the British Navy like those other 'lively little lads in Navy Blue.' Ordinary folk could spare scant time to think of the world's great events. Many had lost loved ones in the seventy wars of Victoria's sixty glorious years, and yet there was a feeling still hanging over all that war was glorious and that war was inevitable.

Would it be against the Russians? The French? The Germans? That was the only query - against whom? If Mary did think somewhat cynically of the great red Empire on the world's map, she was at the same time honest enough to admit that it was probably better to be British than to be anything else; and that, if the British were colonisers, they were certainly the most decent and well-meaning yet seen in the world's history. Early in life, Mary found herself in a minority of one. She was anti-war in an age when this was an unfashionable attitude. In spite of her own belligerent nature, she was a pacifist. She had a bad habit of seeing two sides of an argument. To be honest, she had occasionally an even worse habit of seeing only her side, and of being almost viciously bigoted against bigotry. She might have been expected to outgrow such childishness, but somehow she never. did. If she had realised how the black shadows of the Somme hung over the lads in front of her, their heads bowed to their desks or their bare toes touching their chalked semi-circles, she would have been even more anti-war. Instead, she was much more interested in those two lads in Alfred's Great Country who bore a surname common in her school - Wright - but whose given names were so curiously and exotically Ameri-can - Wilbur and Orville. The flying machines had now the magic that had just slightly rubbed off the horseless carriage with a little familiarity. But no one Mary knew had ever seen a flying machine.

Mary admired her Little Sister more and more as time went on. The short-sighted child of Chapter One had become a plump, pretty girl of fourteen-going-on-fifteen by the time Mary's Finals came round. Little Sister knew she couldn't see very well, but then she never had done - not since her childhood measles that had made her so very ill. She had compensatingly wonderful hearing and musical qualities of genuine talent. Mary's hearing was all right, but she did envy Little Sister her talent. All the family knew that their parents had regarded music, poetry, art and dance as essential units of education. Sometimes Mary thought, 'If only ...' And it was always, 'If only Pappy and Mother had lived, we would have ...' and then she would spin a wonderful dream. But she rarely thought thus, for it was a pointless exercise. Much better for the children to try to do as their parents would have wished, especially things they enjoyed themselves.

Alfred as a young boy had been the first to be sent for

dancing lessons. Each week the dancing master arrived. He came to the house where Mr William John Ferguson's mother still lived. This house was somewhat curiously called 'The Nursery,' Mary never knew why. Old Mrs Ferguson, the grandmother of Kathleen, Molly and Leeby, was an overpowering personality, who was always referred to as 'The Big Mistress.' William John had, by this time, his own fine new house, Oakmount, hard by the ancient Holestone, but his older children and the children of minor gentry and of farmers round-about congregated at the Big Mistress's weekly to learn their one-two-three-and-a-hop, or their simple one, two, rise. All the Bridge children were musical except Mary, who loved music so but was No Performer. Mother died when Mary was very young, and yet the little girl could remember her mother taking her and Lennox and Alfred to one of the cotter houses where a new resident purported to be a teacher of singing. Mary even remembered his arms waving wildly as he intoned, Doh, Ray, Me, and made the infant children repeat this after him. It was evidently not quite true that he was the follower of Saint Cecilia he claimed to be, and Mary was not so young that she couldn't remember her little mother putting her hand swiftly over her mouth, so that the man's feelings might not be hurt by an unavoidable smile.

Little Sister was 'discovered,' to use a later idiom, when she was only five years old. Mary was sent to Mr Tom Bailie's singing class in the Torrens Hall in Doagh on Saturday mornings, and Little Sister went along for the ride. Mr Tom Bailie was the Master of Ballyeaston National School and Precentor of First Ballyeaston Presbyterian Church, an excellent teacher and a fine and talented musician. With his long beard, he looked like an energetic musical Santa Claus. Mary always remembered the charming story of Mr and Mrs Bailie (who also taught in Ballyeaston School), keeping the wooden cradle of their first born beside the schoolroom fire where the parental foot could rock it.

When Mr Bailie heard Mary's Little Sister singing, he was thunderstruck. The tiny voice was perfectly in tune and had a volume and quality that was almost adult. So delighted was he by this discovery, that he took the child's hands in his and waltzed her round and round the Hall in her little red coat. Mary admired her too and was not at all envious, basking in her reflected glory. From Mr Bailie, Little Sister learned the first songs that made her an infant prodigy in appearances at half-hour concerts at bazaars, box teas, basket teas and church swarrys (soirées). It was not until she was nine years old that

170

she was sent with Mary for their first pianoforte lessons from Miss Cis Beggs, whose family kept the pub in Burnside, and whose orchard was an autumnal magnet for those naughty children who robbed orchards in the wrong way. There was a definite ruling about the right and the wrong ways of going about this popular juvenile crime, just as there was about birds nesting. You could take an apple or an egg, provided you broke no branches and destroyed no nests or young.

Even at ten shillings for the term of thirteen lessons, the little girls made but scant progress. They did, however, arrive at a business arrangement between themselves. Little Sister was so short-sighted that she found difficulty in reading the notes on the lines and spaces. Mary knew the notes immediately, but was, as we have already noted, No Performer. So while she read the notes, Little Sister quickly learned and performed them. Mary's stiff fingers now determined that she was No Pianist. But hold! Worse was to follow!

When their first attempts at mastering the pianoforte came to little, the travelling music teacher, Mr Brown, was engaged to teach them at home. He was an excellent musician and, more unusually, a fine teacher of music. He had only one little weakness that was as endearing as it was occasionally deplored. Organist and Precentor in Parkgate Presbyterian Church Sunday by Sunday, he had to pass along much of the route he travelled on week days from his home at Ballycorr. When it reached the Doagh Hotel, his pony stopped by itself and took the trap and Mr Brown into the pub yard willy-nilly. The poor man had often great difficulty in persuading the beast that the Sabbath was not made for man in quite this way.

Everything Mary learned about instrumental music, she learned from Mr Brown. Her learning was limited only by her own lack of talent, for she did try. But Little Sister glided placidly on taking everything in her stride, and easily reproducing not merely notes and time, but the technique Mr Brown required. Mary thought she herself was lucky to acquire the rudiments. Mr Brown had a kind heart for Mary. He must have realised what a struggle it was for her, for he went out of his way to be helpful, even though his helpfulness took odd forms. Little Sister continued singing lessons with him and he tried Mary at singing too. He always called her 'Flora, My Flower,' with old-fashioned gallantry. His gallantry was sorely tired, however, when he first asked her to sing. She did her usual best, which was frightful. He gazed sadly at her over his spectacles for a few moments before commenting, 'Flora, My Flower, I

171

don't understand at all why you can't sing, for a small mouth is no use.' This, understandably, made Mary No Singer for the rest of her life!

Mr Brown had two real claims to fame, however, which he never failed to bring into the conversation that larded his lessons.

'Did I ever tell you young ladies,' he would say, 'how I brought the Ulster Hall down?' The way this question was posed, together with the frequency of its utterances, made the bringing-down of the Ulster Hall a trial to Mary's solemnity. But his other gambit held real, glamorous interest.

'Did I ever tell you young ladies that my dear wife is a cousin of Dame Clara Butt?' At this time, the great contralto was at the height of her powers, and Mr Brown felt that Little Sister had the brilliant talent to emulate that Diva. He wished for her a great future.

Soon, poor Mr Brown was involved in an accident. He sustained a broken leg and other injuries which quite put an end to his career as a travelling teacher. Thus Little Sister progressed to the more advanced teaching of Mr Charles Lindop, at that time organist in Antrim Parish Church, and about to become one of Belfast's leading musical Lights. When she felt she had absorbed all Mr Lindop had to offer, she progressed further to Mr Clavering Archer who specialised in opera and oratorio; and from him to a rising young musician called Charles Brennan. From each teacher she got a different emphasis - articulation and diction, bel canto, interpretation, repertoire, variety of musical taste, harmony and musical form until finally, Miss Orr-Owens (last head of that great family of Holestone House), offered to send her to London for her artistic polishing and a career on the concert platform. It was only at this point that Little Sister, after long searching thought, decided to remain in Ireland. Whether she made the right or wrong decision, who can now tell? It might have been better for herself if she had gone to London. It would certainly have impoverished the musical life of her native land and been a real blow to her huge circle of friends and acquaintances.

The curious reader will ask how a little girl, living in such conditions of near-to-the-bone genteel poverty, ever afforded lessons from such recognised masters of her day. She was a singer first, then a good interpretative pianist and a more than competent organist. She knew her talent early in life, and herself decided to do all she could to better her condition. So to get lessons for herself, she gave lessons to others. It was simple logic and an immediate answer to her problem. It also showed her early intelligent application of common sense to everyday living, for at the age of twelve years she took her first three pupils at home in Bridge House, and thereafter for fifty years never ceased to learn or to teach.

When she started at twelve, she could see enough to manage her three almost-grown-up pupils and to master the new art of teaching. One eye that was weaker than the other deteriorated rapidly under the strain, but she was left with faint sight in it and reasonable sight in the other. What terrible tricks fate can play on us all! When she married, during the First World War, she and her husband started to lay out the Bridge House gardens anew, for they had a love of growing things. A coil of wire to enclose a new plot lay on the ground like a malevolent snake ready to strike. The simile was only too apt.

'Hold that end,' said Tom, 'while I unroll it,' and he went off up the garden, whistling, uncoiling the wire as he went. How it happened no one would ever know exactly, whether something startled this dear Little Sister, or whether the turning wire in her hand wriggled out of her grasp. But, snap! went the vicious free end of the wire, coiling upwards from her hand to her face and slashing her across the wide-open good eye. Does such a horrible turn of fate seem possible? Can anyone ever understand why such a thing should have happened to a Little Sister who had already had to struggle so gamely with life?

To pass over such a terrible time quickly is the only thing possible. The young bride, through anguish that was both physical and mental, not only came, through great strength of faith, to reconcile herself to everlasting darkness, but to make of her life an example of spirited bravery to others, and a fountain of lively entertainment to her friends and her public. No words are sufficient to pay tribute to her. And, after all, perhaps Providence had sent that pale little baby to Bridge House long ago when Aunt Laetitia just somehow had to manage to care for her. For Moxie remained loyal and steadfast and unselfish, caring for the handicapped one of the family that had first held out loving hands to her.

Out in the great big world that Little Sister might so easily have graced, Edward and Alexandra held brilliant Court. Gone were the days of rigidity and pietistic values of that old Queen who, just before Mary became a Monitress, had died in the loving embrace of her dear grandson, the German Kaiser. Not yet come were the serious and decorous years of George and Mary, who would teach the world to do its duty, even while giving a slight impression of having a Royal eye to the main chance, along with some heritage of Victoria's 'jealous grip on prerogatives.' Monitress Mary's little reign in the Cogry Mills' School, her teenage years, lay wholly within the randy rule of Edward. And she was never sorry that this was so. Nor that Sipido's bullets in Brussels had passed between the two Royal heads instead of through them. If Ireland had to have some nominal rulers, she felt that these were, at least, an interesting pair, one a Merrie Monarch, the other a Beautiful Queen. In the year that launched Mary as a Monitress, Edward and Alexandra flitted to Buckingham Palace, all newly-got-up in Alexandra's taste, which was *bound* to be better than Victoria's. The new lovely Queen was sadly deaf; was, apparently, not very bright; but certainly had style, just as Edward had charm. Mary reckoned that they must have lived in a fashion that would not have been tolerated by Aunt Laetitia, when she heard that the Duchess of York wrote to her husband George that Marlborough House, left by the Royal Pair for the young 'uns to inhabit, was unsuitable.

'I hope your father was not very angry with you about Marlborough House,' wrote the upright Royal Mary. 'That question quite weighs on my mind, as surely he must know we really cannot go into a filthy dirty house - not even to oblige him!' However, in our Mary's first year, the Royal Mary got her new home cleaned to her satisfaction, furnished it elegantly in her own excellent taste, and bought the young pair's first motor car. Edward and Alexandra's first car was already two years old, the Royal homes had just installed telephones, all the Royals had been to see the cinematograph, the younger fry had listened by courtesy of the G.P.O. and the new electrophone to operatic performances, and the German Count Zeppelin had invented an airship. The German Count and, indeed, the Teutonic-English Royal Family would not have been so pleased with all this progress in time, had they realised that it had brought to birth another lad, a scant nine months younger than our Mary, the third child of a third marriage, whose name was Adolf Hitler. Certainly, Grannie Mellon would have been driven to wonder at last if three were really the lucky number she believed it to be!

It was not only the Royals who had their social whirl. That winter of nineteen hundred and seven brought Mary more outings. True, they had few diamonds, no champagne whatever, and very little gambling. Nonetheless, gambling of a kind was part and parcel of any bazaar.

174

The Parish Church of Saint Bride required no funds, for usually the Rector, like most Rectors of his time a scholar and a gentleman, dipped in his own well-lined pocket. But for Presbyterian reasons, not the least of which was entertainment, the Master had decided upon a Grand Christmas Bazaar and Sale of Work in aid of his favourite African Mission to the Iboes. As this was a Christian function, shooting, bean bag throwing, guessing the weight of a cake or any other activity that a Jew might have considered a game of chance, became instead a game of skill to these Christians. And present they were in their hundreds in the Torrens Memorial Hall.

Weeks, even months, had gone into the preparations for the big event, which was scheduled for the Friday night before Christmas. All devotees of the Mission Hall, and all compulsory devotees, had worked hard since the coming of Isaac among them. Isaac was a magnificent Iboe who had been adopted and educated by the Master's mission public. Finishing his education in London, Isaac was himself about to return to his own people as a Christian missionary, but before going back to that hot, barbaric land in very-nearly-darkest Africa, he came to live with the Master and speak to the people who had cared for him. Not only Mary but all those who crowded to see a real live tribal African came under Isaac's spell.

He was as black as your boot, tall and intelligent, his liquid eyes and ebony skin shining above his white collar in the lamp-lit Mission Hall. His soft voice, his peculiar cadences in the English language, his simplicity and nobility, moved those present with a genuine warm impulse to do something for him and his people. Hence the bazaar. Hence Mary, as a compulsory zealot, playing the part of an Irish colleen all togged out in red and green. And well may any reader, gentle or otherwise, ask what on earth an Irish colleen had to do with Africa.

The answer was simple. She was one of the earliest known live models. She represented soap. A firm in Donaghmore, County Tyrone, manufactured this very charming 'Colleen' soap, and had made the Master an outright gift of a large quantity of their product. The money received for the soap would go to the Iboes. The only condition the firm imposed was that it get its full value in advertising. With the load of soap had come a white blouse, a red skirt and a green cloak. It was supposed by someone that all the young girls in Ireland went about wearing such garments. If this were so, then Mary had been to the wrong parts of her country. Now she felt a perfect fright, not to say fool, as she struggled with her basket of soap

175

'He was as black as your boot, tall and intelligent, his liquid eyes and ebony skin shining above his white collar in the lamp-lit Mission Hall.'

through the crowds thronging the bazaar, her green cloak falling over her eyes and half blinding her. The Master noted this disability and kindly left his tea table at the head of the room where the platform party was being entertained. He suggested very firmly to Mary that she throw back her cloak and look where she was going. Feeling now an even more visible fool, she did so. She daren't do otherwise.

But the public was kind. They bought her little bars of soap, each wrapped in olive-green paper with the picture of another fool like herself on it. She was furious but impotent. At last, at last, the final bar of 'Colleen' went, and Mary tottered to the kitchen of the Hall to rid herself of her ridiculous garments, hand over her takings and see something of what was going on. 'Why could they not just have sent the soap itself to the Iboes,' she wondered resentfully and uncharitably.

The Hall, illuminated by eight oil-lamps, wore a highly festive air, where it could be seen at all for the crowds. Earnest ladies, all for some obscure reason wearing hats, sweated over their unaccustomed tasks of selling and of counting change at speed. Beautiful crochet-work and embroidery, dozens of knitted black stockings and socks, sideboard runners and antimacassars disappeared like lightning from the work stall, cakes from the cake stall and groceries from the grocery stall. Children pushed and shoved and importuned parents at the bran tub. Youths concentrated with careful swayings back and forth on throwing bean bags through five holes in a board. Men, awaiting their turn in the shooting contest, shovelled in platefuls of hot peas with vinegar at the hot peas stand. Ladies, as opposed to women, sat down in the small railed-off area near the platform party to have afternoon tea at night. Women, as opposed to ladies, went carefully bargain-hunting, hanging round nearly-empty stalls whose proprietors were about to have a closing-down sale of goods for next-to-nothing; even, if one were lucky, for nothing at all. Mary decided that there was nothing at all in this for her, and that her meagre six-pence should go to the other section of the bazaar held in the Doagh National School across the way.

The other section was pure entertainment. It consisted of a series of half-hour concerts given throughout the course of the evening. Customers in the Hall (which was also the Ladies' School) could, when they had finished buying or when their sore feet became unbearable, pay sixpence at the door of the 'other' school to Beggsie, that ubiquitous door keeper, and have a good sit-down.

They sat in or on the desks according to size and taste and

177

faced the platform. This consisted of a blackboard perilously perched on the backs of several forms. A few artists (or artistes) had undoubtedly been trysted to perform, but Mary had heard committee men in the bazaar importuning those known to have either a bit of talent or a desire for the limelight, urging them to perform in the half-hour concerts.

'Come on on,' a man would say, 'give us a verse. Sure a wee verse o' onythin'll dae. Naebody's carin'!'

This might seem un-encouraging to the purist, but it did produce people willing to oblige. Mary sat on top of a desk at the back of the schoolroom. The light was fitful, coming as it did from borrowed oil lamps, for as a rule a school required no light at night. Here Fred joined her, and brother and sister perched at the back ready to enjoy what the half-hour concert had to offer them. They had little worry about one of the items at least, as their mature fifteen-year-old Little Sister would be singing 'Softly awakes my heart.' That plummy aria which seemed to be the only thing known out of all Saint-Saens' Opera, was a perfect vehicle for her rich sound contralto with its deep tones like a vintage violoncello. To the *hoi polloi*, she would throw an exaggeratedly sentimental 'Home, Sweet Home' *a la* Patti as an encore, and they would cheer to the echo. If pressed, she would give them Tosti's 'Adieu' or 'Thora,' but she was inevitably torn two ways. The serious singer wanted to sing well. The entertainer in her wanted to amuse. Either way, Mary and Freddie paid her little attention and took the audience's adulation for granted. They had heard her whistle and sing ever since they could remember.

The Master's family came out strong on his behalf. His brother Sam gave the audience what they wanted in 'Paddy McGinty's goat' and 'Fitba' Crazy.' Although these were his only songs, they carried him effortlessly through concert after concert and through repeat after repeat, with no diminution in the interest of his warm, live audience. His sister, Lizzie, came out with her one masterpiece too, her own particular kind of lisp adding an entertainment value that was unintentional as she 'looked up and he looked down, handsome sunburnt Johnny Brown.'

Together they remounted the shoogly blackboard for the classic 'Hole in the Bucket,' which always called for its encore, 'The Keys of Heaven.' Having walked and talked successfully through this number, the McNallys descended from the blackboard to make way for a brave child, also called Lizzie, who, taking her life in her feet, raised one arm aloft, one hand on waist, and launched into a lively Highland Fling, while the blackboard bounced merrily up and down on the forms.

The dancer's music having been supplied by the melodeon player, Tommy Agnew, he himself was now permitted a solo turn, and rendered - for no one ever just played or sang - a fittingly lugubrious 'Hame o' Mine,' followed, as was the way, by a contrasting 'Tatter Jack Welsh' that had every toe tapping on the dusty school room floor.

Before Little Sister's item that would close this particular concert, there was just one more, for the audience must not be spoilt. There were three more concerts, all different, to be got through in the course of the evening. That one other item was a performance, by the local dramatic actress, Sarah Martin, of 'Curfew shall not ring tonight,' with its finely-shaped shift of emphasis from word to word as the melodrama of the poem unfolded. Having gone from '*Curfew* shall not ring tonight' to 'Curfew shall not ring *tonight*' in an able manner, with sobbing, throbbing tones and wide-flung gestures, Sarah could usually be persuaded by her good-natured audience to give them that even more cliff-hanging masterpiece, 'Barbara Freitchie.' As 'Barbara' declaimed:

> ' "Shoot if you must this old grey head,
> But spare your country's flag." she said,'

Freddie suddenly leaned over and whispered in Mary's ear, 'If Stonewall Jackson had taken her at her word, she would have got the quare gunk.'

Mary heard no more.

Miss Sarah Martin was not the only dramatic actress round Doagh in the early years of this century. There were dozens. All of them had been drawn to the great arts of drama and speech by the enthusiasm of one young man. He was James Legate, son of the Ballyclare Presbyterian minister. Mary was one among the dozens. Along with her went her nearest friends and rivals in the dramatic world of Doagh - Sarah Martin, Mag Kerr, Fred Shannon, Tommy Allen and that Jim Christie who was to become the next Principal of the Doagh National School. Mr Legate held his classes in the Torrens Memorial Hall. Mary had the benefit, too, of part-time instruction from an up-and-coming young actor who gave speech lessons in Belfast for which Mary saved every difficult penny. This young man's name was McCandless, R H McCandless, who was one of those destined to put Ulster's first very own theatre on the map. And, greatest wonder of all, Mary was about to become positive for the first time in her life.

So far, she had been No Artist, No Needlewoman, No Singer, No-almost-anything-you-care-to-name. At last, she had come into her own. The childhood concerts on the wooden packing case when she, in 'bustle and outsize bonnet with many scarf-drapings' declaimed Shakespeare with enthusiasm but without enterprise, now matured into a life-time's interest. She could act.

Bob McCandless was a fine-featured, powerful young man of great stage presence, with considerable ability in imparting his knowledge of stagecraft to others. He was one of the adjudicators at the many speech and drama - always then called elocution - competitions held in Belfast and throughout the countryside each winter.

It is a very remarkable thing that town dwellers have an opinion of the country that has no justification whatever. This certainly was true in Edward's reign when country life was described as 'dull, colourless and tedious.' Nothing could have been further from the truth. Then, as now, there was no boredom whatever in country life, except for people who carried their own boredom with them no matter where they went. There were no bright lights, it is true. (Len, after staying in Belfast for nearly five years, but visiting home frequently, found it difficult to see 'in the dark' and considered this an excuse to have Jean Herron on one arm and Mary on the other to guide him on his way to a party or concert). But if you needed a light on a winter's night going to any of the many, many types of entertainment available, you could take your hurricane lamp with you to concerts, bazaars, box teas and basket teas, whist drives, parties, 'Catch-my-pal' meetings, magic lantern shows, illustrated lectures, mission hall meetings, balls, soirées, conversaziones, 'Good Templars,' and evening classes in many subjects. Apart from the elocution classes, Mary managed, outside school, to learn French, German and Cookery. Her first Cookery classes were held in 'Farrel's Great Inn' in Doagh village. Tables were set up in the Hunt Room where the 'Pitch Piners' met to socialise. This was the nickname of the local Hunt, revived by self-made merchants in the timber trade, who wished to climb from mere trade into a kind of county bracket. The Hunt in olden days had been financed and run by the Marquess of Donegall. When he became a complete 'Absentee,' all gradually fell into desuetude. The buildings where his fine dogs had been quartered were still 'The Kennels,' but had been turned into a row of little houses.

The elocution classes were Mary's first love. She even forebore at last to laugh at Mr Legate's constant injunction to all his pupils to 'throw your voice to the back of the room!' Instead, she concentrated intently on her text book, Bell's Standard Elocutionist, which was a half-and-half book, the first part being devoted to the acquiring of elocution techniques, the second to a collection of poems and prose, varying in subject and difficulty.

Mary worked on her theory of speech and reading, but with all her learning, she was more of an intuitive actress than an academic. She even found amusement in the Messrs Bell - yes, there were two of them, although the book title gave the impression of there being only one. They obviously had no sense of humour. For their example of 'Emphatic Analysis,' Mr Legate's students worked at 'Lines on the Burial of Sir John Moore.' The Messrs Bell were very keen that students would get their emphasis on the correct words, not, as one would think, in order to make positive sense, but instead to avoid a nonsense that only the Bell brothers would have thought of in the first place. They called it the 'False Antithesis.' Some of these false antitheses were so comical that they intruded into Mary's mind when it should have been concentrating on higher things:

'Not a *drum* was heard ...

The subject *drum* will be accented and the predicate *was heard* unaccented, because the mention of *drum* involves ... hearing. Therefore to accentuate *heard* would involve one of the False Antitheses, for example:

'Not a drum was *heard (because we were deaf),*
Not a drum was *heard (but only seen or felt).'*

Such teaching continued throughout the poem:

'To the *ramparts (not to a cemetery),*
We *buried* him *(instead of leaving him lying on the battlefield),*
Without *bayonets (not with spades),*
But he *lay (instead of assuming some other attitude).'*

The italics are the writer's but the words are the words of Bell. Their 'Power of Poetic Measures' was couched in very Blank Verse:

'Now clear, pure, hard, bright, and one by one, like to

181

hail stones,
   Short words fall from his lips fast as the first of a
      shower:-
   Now in two-fold column, Spondee, Iamb, and Trochee,
   Unbroke, firm-set, advance, retreat, trampling along;
   Now with a sprightlier springiness, bounding in tripli-
      cate syllables,
   Dance the elastic Dactylics in musical cadences on;
   Now their voluminous coils intertangling like huge
      anacondas,
   Roll overwhelming onward the sesquipedalian words.'

One had to be grateful, after reading this mnemonic for the small mercy that the Bell brothers used the poems of others for most of their work.

Gesture and grace were of infinite importance to the elocutionist. It was well for Mary that her gesture and grace were more akin to her dancing feet than to her No Needlewoman hands! She read and learned what was placed before her, but much of her gesture was spontaneous, her grace innate.

'The head should be planted firmly on the neck.' Mary gave hers a tentative shake, but it seemed firmly fixed. So that was all right.

'The feet should stand moderately apart, toes slightly outwards, one foot a little in advance of the other. The weight of the body should be poised on one foot at the time. The supporting limb should be perfectly straight, the knee of the other slightly bent ... the toes turned outwards at an angle of not more than seventy-five degrees'! (All this was a mere bagatelle to a confirmed Lancers dancer!)

Before competition - reciting poems right up to those of great difficulty like 'The Arab's Farewell to his Steed,' 'The Slave's Dream' and Gray's 'Elegy in a Country Churchyard' - Mary revised the twenty-three exercises on articulation, a few of the difficult words and sentences, such as 'Copts,' 'literarily,' 'literally,' 'sects.'

'A shot-silk sash shop.'
'A lump of raw, red liver.'
'I snuff shop-snuff; do you snuff shop-snuff?'
'truly rural.'
'not gamble, but gambol,' 'not holy, but wholly,' 'not idle, but idol,' 'not assistance, but assistants,' - and the final directions for elocution:

182

'Do not stand up hurriedly, or consequentially, or be in haste to begin, but take your position with leisurely grace; pause, and bow before commencing. A few deep inspirations, slowly taken, especially through the nostrils, will assist in subduing nervous agitation. *Realize* everything. Take no further thought of your auditors until the close. Then bow and leisurely (*sic*) retire. Never turn your back on your hearers. Meaningless or indefinite shifts of the head, hands, arms or feet should be carefully avoided. The speaker must learn to ... stand still. Repose is a chief element of effect.'

In spite of her smiles at Bell, Mary never learnt a better lesson than this.

She thought at the time, as Silver Medals and Gold Medals came her way, and gave her her own little niche in the artistic world at last, that she would not soon forget Bob McCandless and James Legate. Perhaps more than either she would remember the brilliant Andy Blair, who would undoubtedly have become yet another of Ireland's many exports of genius, had his life not come to an untimely end. But, she was happy to remember, not before he had had an ideally happy marriage with her pretty young friend, Jean Herron.

Mary did with her Bell's Elocutionist what everyone drunk with poetry does - she read all the poems she didn't have to know, and pre-eminent among her loves was an old, rather poor poem that said something to her of I-know-not-what, that caught her up and in some way brought her near again to Alfred:

> 'It's all very well to write reviews,
> And carry umbrellas, and keep dry shoes,
> And say what everyone's saying here,
> And wear what everyone else must wear;
> But tonight I'm sick of the whole affair.
> I want free life, and I want fresh air;
> And I sigh for the canter after the cattle,
> The crack of the whips, like shots in a battle,
> The melee of horns and hoofs and heads,
> The wars and wrangles and scatters and spreads;
> The green beneath and the blue above,
> And dash, and danger, and life and love.
>
> 'And Lasca! Ah! she used to ride
> On a mouse-grey mustang, close to my side,
> With blue serape and bright-belled spur;

I laughed with joy as I looked at her!
Little she knew of books or of creeds;
An "Ave Maria" sufficed her needs;
Little she cared, save to be by my side,
To ride with me, and ever to ride!
She was as bold as the billows that beat -
She was as wild as the breezes that blow;
From her little head to her little feet
She was swayed, in her suppleness, to and fro
By each gust of passion: a sapling pine
That grows on the edge of a Kansas bluff,
And wars with the wind when the weather is rough,
Is like this Lasca, this love of mine.
'She would hunger that I might eat,
Would take the bitter and leave me the sweet;
But once, when I made her jealous, for fun,
At something I'd whispered, or looked, or done,
She drew from her girdle a dear little dagger, and -
    sting of a wasp!
It made me stagger!
An inch to the left, or an inch to the right,
And I shouldn't be maundering here tonight;
But she sobbed - and, sobbing, so swiftly bound
Her torn reboso about the wound
That I quite forgave her. Scratches don't count
In Texas, down by the Rio Grandè!

'One murky night the air was hot,
I sat by her side, and forgot - forgot!
Forgot the herd that were taking their rest;
Forgot that the air was close opprest;
That the Texas "Norther" comes sudden and soon,
In the dead of night or the blaze of noon;
That once let the herd at its breath take fright;
Then - woe to the rider, and woe to the steed
That falls in front of their mad stampede!
Was that thunder? I grasped the cord
Of my swift mustang without a word.
I sprang to the saddle - and she clung behind!
Away! - on a hot chase down the wind!
But never was fox-hunt half so hard,
And never was steed so little spared,
For we rode for our lives. You shall hear how we
    fared

184

In Texas, down by the Rio Grande.

'The mustang flew, and we urged him on;
There was one chance left - and you have but one -
Halt - jump to ground - and shoot your horse;
Crouch under his carcase and take your chance;
And if the steers, in their frantic course
Don't batter you both to pieces at once
You may thank your stars; if not, Good-bye
To the quickening kiss and the long-drawn sigh
And the open air and the open sky
In Texas, down by the Rio Grande.

'The cattle gained on us, and, just as I felt
For my old six-shooter behind in my belt,
Down came the mustang, and down came we
Clinging together - and, what was the rest?
A body that spread itself on my breast.
Two arms that shielded my dizzy head,
Two lips that hard on my lips were prest;
Then came thunder in my ears,
As over us surged the sea of steers.
Blows that beat blood into my ears,
And when I could rise -
Lasca was dead!

'I gouged out a grave a few feet deep,
And, there, in Earth's arms, I laid her to sleep;
And there she is lying, and no one knows;
And the summer shines, and the winter snows;
And for many a day, the flowers have spread
A fall of petals over her head;
And the little grey hawk hangs aloft in the air,
And the sly coyote trots here and there;
And the black snake glides and glitters and slides
Into a rift in a cottonwood tree;
And the buzzard sails on
And comes and is gone,
Stately and still like a ship at sea;
And I wonder why I do not care
For the things that are like the things that were;
Does half my heart lie buried there,
In Texas, down by the Rio Grande?'

Chapter 14

Alfred came home in nineteen hundred and eight. This was the last year of Mary the Monitress. Her brother was surprised and gladdened to see how the thin, pale child he had left five years before had become a self-assured student of nearly twenty. The year was at the early Spring and the family re-union was complete when Lennox was able, in spite of its being the busy season with Mr Magee, to spend an evening at home each week end. It meant a long journey, with much walking when he did not have enough money for all the tram and train fares required. He did not seem to mind just as long as he could sit and listen to this much travelled brother.

Alfred was wearing the good suit he had worn at his departing. It had obviously received little wear and tear. Alfred at work on ranch or railroad had obviously worn other apparel. Now the seams strained a little uneasily as the strong, tall man who had come home stretched an arm or a leg in the suit that had gone away. If the suit was the same, there was other variety in his appearance. The brown eyes twinkled as merrily as ever, but now they flashed their sarky jestings from under a wide-brimmed hat such as Mary had never seen before. It resembled a little the shady straw hats men wore for the hay making, except that it was made of felt instead of straw. It had acquired a jaunty flip to the brim that made it truly Alfred's.

Out of Pappy's cabin trunk came another sartorial wonder - a pair of protective over-trousers.

'Chaps,' Alfred called them, pronouncing a soft 'c.' 'Leather side out in winter. Sheep-skin out in summer. Chaps.'

'Shaps, shaps,' said Moxie softly.

'I guess,' drawled Alfred.

'I dess,' said Moxie.

'I calc'late,' said Alfred.

'I kinkalink,' said Moxie.

'You bet,' said Alfred.

A whole new vocabulary had come to Bridge House, with exciting, dangerous and thrilling descriptions of Alfred's life in the great United States of America. Night after night, week after week, month after flying month, the young people spent all their spare time together. It was almost as though they were together for the last time, thought Mary wonderingly, and then shivered as a goose walked over her grave. Nevertheless, the entertaining Alfred, the bewitched Lennox, the perceptive Mary, the delighted Frederick, the adoring Little Sister, the slightly relaxed Aunt and the jolly Moxie bouncing merrily on the cow-poke's knee as though it were truly a broncho, together they created a picture as beautiful as it was unlikely. Into the small life of an Ulster farm had come the Wild West!

Alfred in Laramie, Alfred in Tucson, Alfred in Cheyenne, Abilene, Douglas, Alfred from Ellis Island to Wyoming and beyond. It could not be so, yet it was so. There were not just new pictures, new clothes, new words, but new songs. Alfred had ever had an ear for a tune and the gift of getting into the company of revellers full of singing. Back to the old country he brought the songs to which Mary would later rock her own babies. Not for her such anaemic airs as 'Rock-a-bye, baby, on a tree-top' or 'Oh, sleep, my baby, you are sharing.' No, never. Her little children fell asleep, placid and happy, to the early American sound of 'Ol' Beebe' and 'San Antonio.'

> 'Ol' Beebe had three full-grown sons,
> Buster, Bill an' Bee,
> An' Buster was the black sheep
> Of the Beebe family.
> They did their best to cure him
> Of his rough an' rowdy ways,
> But at las' they had to git the judge
> To give him ninety days!
>
> *Oh, didn' he ramble, ramble,*
> *He rambled all aroun', in an' out of th' town,*
> *Oh, didn' he ramble, ramble,*
> *He rambled till the butchers cut him down!*
>
> 'He rambled to the races,
> To make a gallery bet,
> He backed a hoss named "Hydrant,"

187

But "Hydrant's" runnin' yet!
He might've had to walk back home,
His frens all frum him hid,
When he chanst to meet ol' George Waddell
An' a dam' good thing he did!

Oh, didn' he ramble, etc.

'He rambled to a swell Hotel,
His appetite was stout.
When he refused to pay the bill
The lan'lord kicked him out.
He went to strike him with a brick,
But when he chanst to stoop,
The lan'lord gave him a kick-in-the-pants
That made him loop-the-loop!

Oh, didn' he ramble, etc.'

Mary was not to know that this would become a precious Negro cult song, its rhythm and tempo those of a forlorn Blues to be sung at black funerals in the far Southland. With Alfred it was a lively, randy song that was made all the more amusing by its quaint words and by his accent, that easiest of all accents for the Ulsterman to acquire. It was to Mary and Lennox all part of that life of adventure and romance that Alfred pictured for them so vividly. Just as delightful to one and all was that other song that purported to portray a little tale of San Antonio. County Antrim men had a partiality for Texas on account of Sam Houston, to say nothing of Jim Bowie and Davie Crockett. The song went with a swing.

'Just as the moon was peeping o'er the hill,
After the work was through.
There sat a cowboy an' his partner Bill.
Cowboy was feelin' blue.
Bill said, "Come down, pal, down into town, pal,
Good time for me an' you!
Don' min' your ol' gal, I know it's col', pal,
If what you say is true."

*"Where is she now?" Bill cried.
An' his pardner jest replied.*

188

> *"San Antone, Antonio,*
> *She hopped upon her pony,*
> *An' rode away with Tony.*
> *If you see her, just let me know*
> *An' I'll meet you in San Antonio!"*

> 'You know the pony that she rode away?
> Thet hoss belonged to me!
> You know the trinkets that she throwed away?
> I was the big Marquis!
> I don' relent it, I might've spent it
> Plunging on Faro Jack,
> An' if she's not happy there with her chappy,
> Tell her I'll take her back!'

> *"Where is she now?"* Bill cried.
> *An' his pardner jest replied.*
> *"San Antone, Antonio,*
> *She hopped upon her pony,*
> *An' rode away with Tony.*
> *If you see her, jest let me know*
> *An' I'll meet you in San Antonio!"*

Throughout these happy evenings of re-union, Alfred thumped out at the old piano an untechnical but satisfactory accompaniment. It was not long before the others could join in Alfred's songs, harmonising and percussing, where suitable, with the poker and tongs, shovel and fire-dogs. The Craigavad company, as well as Stanley, joined in the merriment as often as they could, too, for the jolly, colourful evenings were just the sort they could appreciate. The music ranged far and wide. Little Sister sang for them in her wonderful way and no one moved while that glorious voice held them spellbound. But there was nothing unusual in moving straight from Handel to 'Down at the Old Bull and Bush,' from Mozart to 'Joshua,' for Belfast's Music Hall had taken the Town over and no one who was anyone would admit to not knowing every Cockney or Scots comic on the boards. Ever beloved were Moore's melodies, that curious misnomer, as Tom Moore had never written a melody in his life. But no one cared a fig for that, as they sang the sweetest airs ever to come out of Ireland, set to his words: 'Believe me if all those endearing young charms,' and 'There is not in this wide world a valley so sweet,' and 'At the mid hour of night,' and so many, many more, but especially Pappy's old song, 'Oft

189

in the stilly night.' Everyone now called a piano a 'honky-tonk,' just as they 'guessed' and 'calc'lated' (or 'kinkalinked') all over the place. There was no doubt that the emigrant Alfred had as great a triumph as even he could have wished.

Aunt Laetitia sailed about, no more reconciled to Len's strange friends in their outré clothes. Artists! Artists! She knew what that meant now in these permissive days. She was no fool. She had heard of the doings of such people from the Rector. And he was no fool either. They did have nice manners, she would admit that, but no one who was respectable would dress like *that*. Cloaks, indeed! And wide-brimmed hats! Anyone who was a gentleman would perhaps wear an Ulster or caped coat, and a bowler such as even His Majesty wore, but certainly not these outlandish garments, and above all *not* a scarf tied in a bow! Her small, rather scornful figure became even straighter than usual. Occasionally her small, true voice was heard singing her protest song, that great favourite of her heroine Madame Adelina Patti, 'Home, sweet home.'

Madame Patti's calendar portrait hung in its neat frame above the kitchen mantelpiece. She, like Aunt Laetitia, had an Alexandra fringe and the ubiquitous dog-collar of pearls that gave her an aristocratic air. She, too, looked down a little scornfully at this zany family that could get such zestful enjoyment from the rip-roaring songs of a Wild, Wild West.

As day now succeeded day, Lennie associated less and less with his Craigavad coterie. He loved them and would never forget them but they were growing out of tune with his mood. They had all found their métiers. He still groped blindly for his future. He spent less time even at Herrons', that beloved 'other home.' All his ears and eyes, all his precious minutes were for his elder brother, his childhood hero and now his Svengali. The neglected Mary looked on the two she loved and felt the shadow that was inexorably moving her way. Alone, she stamped her foot with rage, and flung herself on her bed in anguished tears, but always when she came downstairs again, she was composed and outwardly cheerful. Life had had many hard lessons to teach her, but none as hard as this ... that if Lennie wanted to go away, she must make it easy for him, not difficult.

Her dread had its compensation. To forget what was happening to Lennox, she threw herself into the discipline of preparing for her King's Scholarship examination that would crown with glorious success her five years as a student teacher. She hoped.

190

She set her mind on the coming Easter Week.

Concentrating on her Examination subjects certainly gave Mary enough to do. She would be examined in English Etymology and Syntax, English Literature and English Speech. This last subject would be judged mainly by her recitation of any passage (from memory) from her Shakespeare, Goldsmith or Milton that the examiner's fancy dictated. She would be required to pass in Penmanship, using examination paper ruled to normal and to Goliath measurements, doing what the students called among themselves 'big writing' and 'wee writing'. There was nothing like 'big writing' for showing up faults in anyone's hand, for by its means the construction of letters, their comparative heights and the crossing points of loops would be manifest to any Examiner. And Penmanship was only *one* of the 'failing' subjects.

She would further have to apply her Penmanship under the eagle eyes of the Invigilators in Transcription and Dictation, both to be perfect. Nothing less was acceptable.

English, encompassing as it did two of the basic R's, was treated with reverence. Spelling and general handling of the language would be marked from the Student's composed passage on a given topic, the Composition. None of all this caused Mary any great worry. She worked at memorising vast amounts of 'Macbeth,' 'The Traveller' and 'The Deserted Village.'

This was the only real work she had to do in English. Everything else seemed to come naturally, from General and Particular Analysis and Parsing to the utterly correct Penmanship. She plodded on through Birnam Wood and Dunsinane, through Auburn, by 'Lazy Scheldt' and 'Idra's Cliff' until she had made much of great English Literature her own.

Her Reading and Writing having been examined, she would have to submit written papers on the History of Ireland and of Great Britain. She would then have to do huge, hideous and utterly useless 'sums' in Arithmetic and Mensuration, with 'problems' that would well suit an advanced Chess Player. The Geography of the World would present her with another little test, linked to a special paper on the Geography of the British Isles. Having completed all these successfully, she hoped, she would then be faced with her practical subjects. Oh, dreaded hours! When they should arrive, she would faint. She would die. She felt certain of it.

Half a morning spent on Art! For someone who had been No Artist from an early age, the idea was torture. There was something called Mechanical Drawing that the Master had taught her. She never did know what it was all about, but followed blindly the lead set her. She would also be faced with Object Drawing, not from objects at all but from a drawing on a card. 'Right,' she thought, 'I'll copy it as closely as possible. It can't be all that bad.' She prayed as never before.

Her Practical Music Examination would take place in her own school. The itinerant Inspector heard all the young ladies and gentlemen aspiring to be teachers. They couldn't teach if they couldn't sing. It was as blunt as that. No rhyme. No reason. Just sing or else. Mary was No Singer, but she could follow the Master's pointer as it hopped about up, down - yes, and across - the Modulator. The Master showed a kind of grim satisfaction with her efforts. It was as though he said clearly, 'You're a rotten singer but you can hit a note right in the middle.' As with the Modulator, so she concentrated on her Sight Reading. She had to be immediately conversant with both Staff and Tonic Solfa and interchange the two, and many a time she had reason to rise up and call Mr Brown blessed, despite the pub-crawling pony. Her written paper would be done in Easter week, at the final King's Scholarship Examination.

Having decided just what, with the Master's willing help, she could actually do reasonably in the way of preparation for her Examination, she was left with the unreasonable - Domestic Economy. Heaven knew, her life had been boringly Domestic, to one who wished above all to travel to Egypt to see the Pyramids, and to China to see the Great Wall. And certainly, never since the children had been orphaned had they known anything but the most rigorous Economy. But somehow these two facts gave Mary no help at all in her preparation for this rigorous and 'failing' subject - and part of it was that haunting Needlework. Thank Heaven, they couldn't yet enforce Practical Cookery as so few schools had any cooking stove or other equipment.

Head in hand Mary conned her book fiercely, concentrating so hard that Lennox and Alfred could not enter her conscious thought.

'Those things which we take to flavour our food are known by the name of *Condiments*. Those principally used are: (i) saline substances; (ii) acidulous substances; (iii) oily substances; (iv) saccharine substances; (v) aromatic and pungent substances.'

Mary rhymed this over and over. Such rubbish! Why couldn't they say salt, vinegar, oil, sugar, spice and have done with it? Substances indeed! She rhymed on. Only the given word could be given back on an examination paper. Miss E Rice, late Mistress of Method and Lecturer on Domestic Economy at Cheltenham Training College for Mistresses, had spoken. Miss E Rice was a very funny lady indeed, though, to be fair, often quite sensible too. Sometimes one couldn't be quite sure which cap she was wearing at a given moment, viz., 'Hysteria is said to live and grow on Superabundant Sympathy. Patients will soon recover if removed from kind friends. It often owes its origin to physical disorders but weakness of willpower has a great deal to do with it. The manifestations of feeling(?) called the "hysterical fit" of either laughing or crying, must never be encouraged. A sponge full of cold water applied to the head and back of the neck will cut short an attack.

'With children a decided manner tends to prevent a seizure.'

Mary was often carried away by interesting passages like the above instead of concentrating on Prehension, Mastication, Insalivation, Deglutition, Chymification and Chylification. Who wouldn't? Especially when you could get away from Prehension, etc., by reading up 'Temperance' in the same text book, and find out something about yourself.

'The strong feeling of disapprobation at that which is wrong is a very different thing from passionate anger. To lose one's temper is unmanly or unwomanly and is also seriously detrimental to the digestive organs.'

Mary could expect a good strong onslaught of indigestion any of these days, she thought grimly.

She ploughed on through Nitrogenous and Carbonaceous Foods, the Effect of Clothing on Health, Drainage, Mortgages, Epilepsy and Erysipelas, Leguminous Plants, Impure Air, Washing Flannels, Scrubbing Wood, Making Bread - always Yeast, never, never Soda Bread or Tatie Farls or anything one might actually use - How to clean the grate, Economical Puddings. Mary learnt her book off by heart, even though she would never expect to treat 'poisoned wounds caused by the bites or stings of snakes or of poisoned arrows,' any more than she expected 'to take care not to speak of our savings to strangers as there are always designing people about to pounce upon the unwary'!

In spite of her occasional hilarity at Miss E Rice's vast knowledge, Mary was sober immediately when faced with that other science, Needlework. She appealed frequently to Miss Allen now, day after day, for work to do in knitting and sewing. She asked constant questions about the Examination itself, the form it would take, down to the last detail of what would be required of her, so as to familiarise herself completely with her ordeal.

'Now, now, don't worry,' said Miss Allen. 'You'll get into a state and then you won't even be able to thread the needle.'

This was a worry Mary hadn't yet considered. She added it to her list.

'It's simple,' went on Miss Allen. 'Not easy, but simple. Now make sure of your *proportions*. After that it's plain sailing. You won't fail. I can almost promise you that. Stop making a mountain out of a molehill.'

Mary didn't let her kind, ever-patient instructress know that she didn't make a mountain of it. She built a complete range of Himalayas instead.

'Now remember,' said Miss Allen for the hundredth time. 'Specimens first, then your sock, then your shirt. Take one thing at a time, and don't panic. Make sure you get your *proportions* right. That *is* vital.'

And having cheered Mary up thus, Miss Allen started off yet again to take her through her specimens, while her pupil, stupefied, wondered how you could take two things at a time in Needlework.

At the Practical, Mary would do her specimens - and specimens they would be. A large square of calico would be stamped with her Examination Candidate's Number. Then, on this material she would give ten samples of her craft - Running, Hemming, Back-stitching, a Run-and-Fell seam, a French seam, a Round-end Buttonhole, a Squared-end Buttonhole, a Patch, Tucking and Gathering. A little piece of knitted material with a hole and her number would provide her with the very situation in which to show off how well she could darn.

Before the examination she would have to knit on four shiny steel needles a little sock as far as the heel. The inexorable rubber stamp would mark its ownership, and Mary would have to take up her baby sock then and there in the Examination Room and turn its heel, knit its foot and 'take it off' at the toe.

Finally, the real test - The Great Trial - The Shirt.

It was because of the Shirt that Miss Allen kept on and on about Proportions. In the actual Practical, one could be asked to make a shirt full-size, half-size or quarter-size.

The shirt was, naturally, an Ideal Shirt for a perfectly proportioned man. If you could learn the ideal neck size, sleeve size, cuff size, yoke size, length and breadth, you could, if pushed, divide by two or by four. Thus, if your memory held out, you would at least get your shirt the right size.

Secretly, Mary at last determined on a sin. It was so important to her, this examination. It meant her whole life. If she failed in her Shirt, she had no future. All of this was no excuse. She determined to write the ideal man's proportions under her blouse cuff. (And she did!)

Having by knavery got the shirt the correct size, she reasoned she would be all right with the seams, sleeves, yoke and cuffs. She would remember Miss Allen's delicate instruction, 'Don't forget, dear, to make the back longer than the front. We must remember - ahem! - there's more *space* to cover.' Would that be enough for a Pass Mark? She doubted it, sitting on her bed learning for dear life, literally. She must, just must, get the front band on and do its buttonholes. She must somehow gather the front and back on to their yokes. She must do her facings and bindings. How in Heaven's name would she get the ghastly neck band stitched and turned neatly in place? Underneath this panic was a great and legitimate resentment. She could do it. She knew she could make a shirt now. Not a very good shirt, but wearable. If only *they* would give her a piece of material.

But the really hideous thing was that her shirt, quarter size though it might prove to be, would have to be made from strong, unpliable, cream coloured sheets of good quality paper!

Easter, nineteen hundred and eight, came at last. Before the King's Scholarship Examination should begin on Easter Tuesday, before the religious joys of Easter Sunday and the secular pleasures of Easter Monday should arrive, one had to pass through the oppressive sorrows of Holy Week in the empurpled Church. These rose to their climax of grief on the curiously-named 'Good' Friday and fell suddenly to the Limbo of a Saturday that was neither good nor bad but seemingly indifferent. That is, until everyone who could went along to the Church in the evening bearing flowers, as the Rector bore his festal colours, to make the lovely little building glorious for the dawning of Easter Day.

Mary, Alfred, Lennox, Frederick and Little Sister were able to use the six-year-old Moxie as their excuse to return for a little while to their own childhood pleasures. Mary went to the hen-house where Aunt Laetitia now kept only a dozen birds with their one attendant highly-coloured rooster. These were sufficient to supply the family with boiled, fried, scrambled, coddled or poached eggs, with baked custards and with enrichment for the occasional seed cake, pudding or plum-duff. From untenanted boxes, she took the cooling eggs that had shells shading from chalk white to speckled brown, so variegated was their parentage. She shoved cross parturient hens aside to grope underneath them for their own eggs or the eggs of other hens left there earlier, all warm from the plump feathered bodies. Her booty she carried back to the house to be prepared on Saturday for eating on Easter Monday.

In the meantime, Little Sister and Moxie went with Alfred to acquire whin blossoms and scratched hands. Frederick kindly made himself responsible for collecting all used tea-leaves from this and the previous day. Lennox coaxed from Aunt Laetitia a scrap of red flannel from a good piece of worn petticoat set aside for patching another. With Mary's trophies and their primitive dyes they all set to work, Moxie no less interested and excited than the others in spite of her allergy to eggs.

The white eggs were hard-boiled with the red flannel to produce rosy-pink and crimson eggs. The whin blossoms, boiled · with the faint-coloured eggs, gave varying delicious shades of creamy yellow. The tea leaves, already used but not spent, were boiled with the brown eggs to produce attractive coffee and chocolate eggs. Now came the fun.

Mary had been made well aware from earlier days that she was No Artist. Nevertheless, with Len now to help, she could draw upturned mouths, startled eyebrows, much-fringed eyes and straight lines for noses, with anyone. Fred set some of them in a row in all the available egg cups, looking for all the world like so many little Humpties. Alfred's big brown hands pleated dainty white ruffs from the margin of the *Belfast Telegraph*, so that coloured eggs could sit in these as in so many Shakespearean collars, while for their heads it took the small fingers of Moxie and Little Sister to fashion paper hats. Then they, too, sat in their row like little Easter people. Moxie was enchanted, despite the fact that she could never, never eat the eggs themselves. Everyone else, from Aunt Laetitia to Little Sister, would eat them all up when they had been ceremonially broken. Such splendid eggs were not for eating at a hum-drum breakfast table. No, indeed.

On Easter Monday, in the middle of the afternoon, the basket of gaily coloured eggs was carried by Alfred to the top of the Big Field. Moxie and Little Sister and Carlo circled like mad March hares round and round the others on their way. Alfred laid down this festive burden by the mossy bank at the head of the field. Here was a slope sufficient for the job. Len spread a carriage rug for his Aunt. She seated herself graciously. Fred set beside her another basket containing bread and butter sandwiches, a twist of paper containing salt, and mugs for drinks of

Eiffel Tower lemonade. The trundling began.

Their Aunt and Carlo looked benignly on from the rug as all six started rolling their eggs downhill. The little slope was barely sufficient for a really good run, but someone called Alfred seemed to have placed a few stones in strategic spots so that soon the first egg was cracked. Little Sister and Moxie ran with it to Aunt Laetitia who gave them a pinch of salt and some bread and butter. Moxie confined herself to this last, but pursued the game of egg trundling with lively joy, her little thin legs flashing under her heavy skirts as she pursued her next victim downhill. Not a whit behind her in enjoyment were her grown-up cousins. One would have thought they had never seen an egg before, so noisy was their pleasure, so great their delight, so innocent their rowdiness as a cream, rose or chocolate egg rolled smack! into a cunning stone.

At last there were no more eggs. Fred absentmindedly finished up the bread and butter. With more noise than was seemly, the boys drank all the lemonade.

'Shift,' said Len to Carlo, who moved unwillingly from his comfortable rug. Len and Alfred stretched themselves on the rug by their Aunt, gazing up into the forget-me-not sky with its few baby puffs of white cloud. Moxie and Little Sister sat on the grass, trying to put some of the Humpties together again. Mary wandered by the mossy bank. She would always remember that it was a hot day. Easter could bring any sort of weather, from snow-storms to a pet day like this. She gathered the first primroses from the bank and thought of the morrow. The morrow for her would really begin tonight, when she would entrain at Doagh Upper Station on the Broad Gauge railway to Belfast.

At the kind invitation of Fred's Winifred's family, she would stay with them throughout this examination week. The Examinations were to take place in the Belfast Model School on the Falls Road. Mary looked forward to the ride there and back every day on the horse-trams. She looked forward to having a good close look at the new City Hall, opened by Edward and Alexandra at the same time as Ballyclare had opened its wee old school as a Council Chamber, at the same time as Mary had bought her Donegal tweed that was still her 'best' coat. She looked forward to nothing else.

Model Schools were not model schools. They were merely so called because they were all attached to a Teacher Training College, and provided student teachers with opportunities for teaching Model Lessons. Their name had, however, over the years, come to mean something quite different. They had a conscious air of superiority ingrained in their very red-brick walls. Anyone who either learned or taught in a Model School was, it was firmly believed, a cut above everyone else.

Mary looked down at her new clothes. She had such wealth this Final Year! Sixteen whole Pounds! She had bought her Easter finery herself, and she would wear it to the Examinations - a hyacinth-blue blouse with a skirt to match. Just under the long cuff of the left sleeve, she would write on her arm the dreaded Proportions. Come Friday, that is. She had made up her mind to sin. And not to repent. Whatever happened.

She turned at the end of the field and wandered back in the hot sunshine with her posy of primroses. All the family was there, on or around the carriage rug, every one she loved gathered in one place. She stood and looked at them for a long time. Alfred moved her.

'Mosey along, there!' he shouted. 'Yippee!'

A wet July came after a hot June. Holidays were here again. Although the laurels and flowering currants in the front garden dripped with soft summer rain, Mary disregarded them daily. She was watching each morning for the postman, trudging on his long morning round, never bringing her the letter she awaited. Sometimes she walked in the rain - she had always loved walking in the rain, even in that thundery rain that drove Aunt Laetitia to hide in the little cloakroom under the stairs - to the garden gate. The sweetbriar there cast clouds of invisible fragrance all round her as she waited. To her mind came unbidden the words of Milton, not by any means her favourite poet:

'Fragrant the sweet earth after soft showers.'

Hush! Was that a sound? No. Nothing but the drip of rain from rose leaf to rose leaf.

But, like all things, in its due time her letter came. She had passed! Passed! Passed! And not just Passed, but Passed in the First Division, the highest group of all. She executed a war-dance up the garden path, screaming like a mad thing. Her aunt, sister and cousin came running to the Hall door, wide-eyed, sane enough to keep in out of the rain! They could see that she had had good news. They crowded round the soaking, silly girl and kissed and congratulated her heartily. Nothing was lacking from her triumph except that Fred had already left for his office, and Alfred and Lennox were both at Len's place in Town. They had been there now for three weeks, but were expected on Saturday. This was only Thursday. How could she wait two whole days? If she hadn't felt unable to face the look on Aunt Laetitia's face, she would have sent a telegram. Instead, she got everyone organised, preparing for a Festival Homecoming, herself for once cast as the Birthday Girl.

They swung up the back lane together, the brown-eyed brothers, laden with suitcases and paper parcels. Moxie was waiting for them, her chin resting on a bar of the back gate. They had no free arms in which to carry her, but she trotted along happily between them, holding on to a coat tail on either side.

'My, oh, my,' said Alfred, when he saw the dining room table. 'Whew!'

'Many, many, happy returns,' said Len, inspired.

Mary stood, rosy with pride and modesty. Her table did look well. It had taken them all day to make it so beautiful. She and Little Sister both nodded and smiled. Then they shook their heads, signifying that there was something else to come. The dawn broke on both brothers at the same moment, and they pounced on Mary and lifted her, screaming with partly-real fright, up on to their shoulders where they bounced her merrily. Moxie and Little Sister screamed and danced too. Fred clapped and whistled shrilly, over and over again. Aunt Laetitia put her hands over her ears and commanded silence at least twenty times before she got it and everyone was settled at the pretty birthday table.

'Oh, great, great,' said Alfred. 'I'll miss all this. You just don't know how much I'll miss it.' And his voice and manner were as soft as Mary had ever known them.

'Now, don't be silly, Alfred,' said Mary, gentle and cheerful. 'You don't have to miss it. You just stay and you'll have it. Always.'

'No go, sister,' said Alfred. 'But you're right. I'll admit, you're right. I would always have it. But first I must see all I can see. An' I'm gonna do all I can do.'

'I just do not know, Alfred, why you want to be so *uncomfortable*,' said Little Sister sagely. 'You know, I like to hear the stories, but I don't think I would really like all that wrangling or whatever you call it.'

'Mangling,' said Moxie helpfully, nodding her head brightly.

'Do be quiet,' said Little Sister. 'Wrangerling then, and ... bossing about on railroads ... and people really shooting ... and ... and ... all the other things.' She ended lamely, suddenly

199

remembering that Aunt Laetitia was in their midst, who had not heard by any means all of Alfred's escapades.

'I'm going too,' said Len.

The words fell like three separate thuds on a drum. Mary wasn't even sure for a moment that she had heard them. Then she knew she had. She had been waiting for them. Somebody was shouting - 'No, No, No, No, No, No ...' over and over again. Aunt Laetitia suddenly leaned over the table, and, in spite of her age and trembling hands, slapped Mary very hard on the cheek. The 'No, No' stopped. Mary felt very dull and weary. Into her mind came Miss E Rice and something about a cold wet sponge. Her eyes were fixed on the wholesome Birthday Cake. They had never once had pink butter since - when - oh! ever so long ago. She supposed without interest that they wouldn't be having it again.

Mary could not bear the confines of the house. Her heart was too full. Her mind was distracted. They were gone. Never, never would she see them again. She would never, never care about anything again in all her life.

And, oh, not for nothing either had that faraway look of anticipation appeared in the dreaming eyes of Frederick.

She knew as surely as though she were clairvoyant that soon, so very soon, the terrible scourge of loss by emigration would have robbed her life of all its menfolk. It was not to be borne. Tears blinded her as she walked fiercely down the back lane and on to the road. She dashed a hand across her eyes, caring not who saw her. Before her stretched the beauty of the tree lined avenue. There was their dear little bridge over their own river. The river, like her life, was grey today. By Drumadarragh, the silver curtain of approaching rain showed, faint as a moth's wing. She sat on the bridge and was glad of it. Pour, rain. Run, river. You are right to weep.

Rage possessed her àgain. She cared not a fig for her fine Results now. Her Examination at last meant nothing at all. Nothing. Damn Examinations. Damn J.P. Damn everything. She kicked the bridge and the cold grey stones hurt her for her folly. She wickedly wished she hadn't passed. Then they would have had to stay and look after her instead of deserting her. Oh, Alfred. Oh, dear, dear Len. How could you?

She took another tizzy of rage and wished ferociously that they hadn't had the comfort of knowing she was safe. If only they had suffered instead of poor Pappy who really did love her, and who had died not knowing she would be all right. They

' "You're John, aren't you?" she said. '

should have suffered as she was suffering now. She leaned over the bridge, her tears falling to swell so very imperceptibly the summer flood of swirling water.

A touch on her ankle did not even make her start. She was too miserable, too sunk in self-pity, to mind. She glanced down uncaringly. Two brown eyes looked up at her, merry, questioning eyes. They belonged to a little dog.

'Hullo, dog,' said Mary dully, and turned again to look over the darkening fields, full of summer riches, to the Church on the hill. The little dog limped round and sat down by her other foot that hung in its listless black boot by the bridge wall. She knew the little dog. Poor little lady! She had been hurt in some accident and went through life cheerfully on three legs and a stump. What business had she to be merry with such a loss? Mary had known her owner too, one of those big boys like Frederick who had done Mensuration and such-like esoteric masculine subjects with the Master. The boy had salvaged the little creature and cared for it, giving it the foolish, affectionate name of Norah.

Mary almost smiled for a moment as she thought of it, for it brought to mind the daft nick-names among those big boys who were of her own age group - John Cousins, always 'Goosie' Cousins since he asked out each morning to feed his pet goose; and 'Daddy' Wright, a lanky lad who had lost part of his name over the years as it was reduced from Daddy-Long-Legs; and this other lad whom the others poked fun at as 'Three-legged-Norah' for saving this little creature. She put down a hand and stroked the friendly head. Did a little heart's-ease nudge its way into her sorrow at the touch?

Certainly some relief came to her as she looked up to see the dog's owner standing there, looking sympathetic. She supposed everyone knew of her loss. She tried to smile but it was too great an effort. Quickly she turned away again and looked towards the Church. It had disappeared. She blinked. But even with cleared eyes she could see no Church. She had not realised that the rain was raining on all three of them. Mary and the merry little dog and the young man.

Silently and seriously he was knotting his white linen handkerchief at each of its four corners. With a chivalry worthy of a Raleigh, he held the head-cover out to the girl. She took it, and with no sense of the ridiculous sat on the bridge with it on her head.

'You're John, aren't you?' she said.

'Yes,' said he. 'I'm John. John McDowell.'